The Work Sampling System®

Omnibus Guidelines
Preschool through Third Grade

The Work Sampling System is an instructional assessment that is used in preschool through fifth grade. Its purpose is to document and assess children's skills, knowledge, behavior, and accomplishments across a wide variety of curriculum areas on multiple occasions in order to enhance teaching and learning.

The Work Sampling System consists of three complementary elements:

1) Developmental Guidelines and Checklist,
2) Portfolios, and
3) Summary Reports.

Work Sampling calls for ongoing assessment that is summarized three times per year. By reflecting classroom goals and objectives, it helps teachers monitor children's continuous progress and places children's work within a broad developmental perspective. Through documenting and evaluating individual performance of classroom-based tasks, Work Sampling strengthens student motivation, assists teachers in instructional decision-making, and serves as an effective means for reporting children's progress to families, educators, and the community.

Omnibus Guidelines

Preschool through Third Grade

4th Edition

Margo L. Dichtelmiller
Judy R. Jablon
Dorothea B. Marsden
Samuel J. Meisels

The Work Sampling System®

REBUS INC, a Pearson Education, Inc. company
New York, New York

For more information about
The Work Sampling System, write to:
Pearson Early Learning
1185 Avenue of the Americas
26th Floor
New York, NY 10036

or call 1-800-435-3085

Preparation of this document was supported in part by a grant from the John D. and Catherine T. MacArthur Foundation. The opinions expressed are solely those of the authors.

DESIGNED AND PRODUCED BY Margaret FitzGerald, Metaphor Marketing Inc.

Printed in the United State of America.

02 01 00   10 9 8 7 6

Part No. 20110 (6/01)
ISBN 1-57212-200-5

Introduction

This volume presents the compilation of the Work Sampling System Developmental Guidelines for preschool through third grade. A companion volume presents the Guidelines for kindergarten through fifth grade. The *Omnibus Guidelines* provides the opportunity to view six years of the Work Sampling System's developmental continuum.

The Work Sampling System's Developmental Guidelines are designed to enhance the process of observation and to ensure the reliability and consistency of teachers' observations. The Guidelines incorporate information from a wide array of resources, including local, state, and national standards for curriculum development. These resources are listed at the end of each volume.

How to read the Guidelines

The Guidelines present each specific skill, behavior, or accomplishment in the form of a one-sentence *performance indicator*. Each indicator is followed by a *rationale* and several specific *examples*. The rationale provides a context that explains the meaning and importance of the indicator and briefly outlines reasonable expectations for children of different ages. The examples show several ways children might demonstrate the skill, knowledge, or accomplishment represented by the indicator. Since different teachers may interpret the same indicator in different ways, the Guidelines promote consistency of interpretation and evaluation across children, teachers, and schools.

Although the examples provided for each indicator suggest a variety of ways that children show their skills and knowledge, they do not exhaust all the ways children demonstrate what they know and can do. The students in any particular classroom may show their knowledge in other ways that reflect their unique backgrounds, interests, and classroom opportunities. We expect that our examples will serve as a catalyst to help teachers think of the range of situations in which children demonstrate specific skills and knowledge, and to understand and evaluate their students' performance within the context of their classrooms. Other examples that are more consistent with an individual teacher's curriculum approach can be added.

In the Guidelines, we have attempted to provide illustrations that are relevant to teachers who work with diverse groups of children. Examples that relate specifically to the development of children with special needs are included to suggest how teachers might assess children with disabilities who are included in regular classrooms. Rather than providing examples related to specific cultural or linguistic groups, we have tried to use inclusive or general language to accommodate children from various cultural, linguistic, economic, and social backgrounds.

The Work Sampling System is a dynamic approach to assessment. It is intended both to inform and reflect best practice. We encourage teachers to use it as a framework for meeting and assessing the needs of all students.

About the Omnibus Guidelines format

Each set of facing pages presents a single performance indicator (along with its rationale and examples) as it progresses through six years. This format allows the examination of the growth and development of a wide range of skills, abilities, and behaviors of children across that six year span.

Each grade level's Guidelines is also published separately in an edition designed to facilitate classroom use. Thus, this *Omnibus Guidelines* is a compilation of six documents, presented in parallel format. The grade level Guidelines contain more examples than are included in the *Omnibus Guidelines*. Most indicators appear in all six grade levels; however, for those that do not, a cross-reference is given if they are incorporated into a related indicator. In a few cases the text notes that no equivalent performance indicator appears at that level. Although indicator numbering is sequential within a single grade, in this edition the same indicator may have different numbering in different grades. Referring to a single grade level indicator by its grade (e.g., Kindergarten), domain (e.g., II. Language and Literacy), functional component (e.g., B. Speaking), and indicator number (e.g., 2) will result in an unambiguous reference (K-II-A-2) that is consistent throughout all the materials in the Work Sampling System.

Our values

Every assessment is guided by a set of values about learning and instruction, and how children should be treated in order to enhance their growth and development. The values of the Work Sampling System are based on the attributes of well-functioning children, as suggested by the work of June Patterson and others. These attributes are that all children can:

• Learn to trust themselves and others;

• Learn self discipline;

- Gain an awareness of others and the ability to feel for and with them;
- Be spontaneous when expressing feelings;
- Become self-reliant and self-starting;
- Become increasingly responsible for their own behavior and safety;
- Develop a sense of humor;
- Form creative ideas;
- Extend basic moving, manipulating, and communication skills;
- Listen with heightened and prolonged attentiveness;
- Acquire factual information, and develop the capacity to conceptualize and represent ideas;
- Have a variety of interests and resources;
- Find pleasure in the process as well as in the product; and
- Show the desire to try, the courage to fail, and the persistence to continue their effort.

We hope that these values will imbue teachers' work with greater professional satisfaction and enhanced learning opportunities for children.

Personal and Social Development

This domain emphasizes emotional and social competence. A teacher learns about children's emotional development—their sense of responsibility to themselves and others, how they feel about themselves and view themselves as learners—through ongoing observation, conversations with children, and information from family members. Teachers learn about children's social competence by interacting with them, observing their interactions with other adults and peers, and watching how they make decisions and solve social problems.

I Personal and Social Development

A Self concept

Preschool-3

1 Demonstrates self-confidence.

Three year olds usually come to school feeling competent, ready to take pride in their ability to do familiar things. However, when the school experience is unfamiliar, young children can be very tentative. After invitations to participate in activities, they usually begin to play with materials and interact with other children and teachers. Three year olds show a positive sense of self by:

- joining other children playing in the house corner, often in parallel play;
- responding to the teacher's greeting and exchanging a few words;
- coming to the snack table and participating in conversations;
- choosing individual activities, such as doing puzzles, painting, or helping to feed the class pet;
- gradually increasing the range and diversity of activities in which they choose to participate.

Preschool-4

1 Demonstrates self-confidence.

Many preschool children come to school with a positive sense of self, certain they will be liked. Others need time to observe and opportunities to learn how to play in a group setting. Confident four year olds will participate in most classroom activities, express emotions, eagerly explore toys and materials, and interact with others in the classroom. They display a positive sense of self by:

- showing excitement when the teacher announces that they will be going on a field trip;
- singing songs at circle time;
- teaching a word in sign language to a classmate;
- entering the dramatic play area and choosing a role that fits the play of others;
- sitting at the art table and exchanging ideas and thoughts, even when the discussion is unrelated to the artwork they are making;
- adapting to playground games and becoming part of the action.

Kindergarten

1 Demonstrates self-confidence.

Self-awareness and positive self-image emerge through interactions with others and through experiences of being effective. Confident five year olds approach new tasks and situations enthusiastically, recognize and express emotions appropriately, and share information about themselves with others. They display a positive sense of self by:

- rushing into the classroom on Monday to tell their teacher and friends about visiting the science museum over the weekend;
- acknowledging sadness about the loss of a pet;
- entering small groups confident they will be accepted after observing for a short time;
- providing a simple explanation about their disabilities to able-bodied children;
- expressing delight over their own very tall block structure and wanting others to like it, too;
- suggesting roles for themselves in dramatic play or the block corner.

First Grade

1 Demonstrates self-confidence.

Self-confidence grows through positive interactions with others and experiences of feeling competent. Most first graders have a "can do" attitude, show satisfaction and pride in their work, and express needs, wants, and feelings readily. Industrious and eager to try new experiences, they sometimes overestimate their abilities and need encouragement from an adult to overcome a challenge. Six year olds display their confidence by:

- choosing a friend with whom to work or play (for example, for partner reading, during choice time, or at recess);
- reading aloud from an unfamiliar book and feeling comfortable about making some mistakes;
- expressing pleasure, without boasting, when selected to work on a new project in the classroom;
- working or playing independently or with a friend without needing frequent adult support or approval;
- coping reasonably well when things do not work out exactly as planned (for example, attempting to build a robot using recycled materials and accepting that it doesn't look exactly like the one in the book).

Second Grade

1 Demonstrates self-confidence.

Self-confidence grows through positive interactions with others and experiences of feeling competent. Many second graders are hard workers who have a tendency to create high expectations for themselves. When the results of their efforts do not match their expectations, they can be quite self-critical. A supportive adult is sometimes needed to guide them past their frustration to a sense of accomplishment. Examples of how they demonstrate confidence include:

- choosing a work or play partner based on friendships or shared interests (for example, someone who likes a particular computer game or is interested in making models);
- asking for help from a teacher after recognizing that a task is too difficult to accomplish independently;
- complimenting a friend's painting without putting down their own work;
- feeling comfortable about selecting a new chapter book from the class library;
- coping reasonably well with not winning a game or not being partnered with a friend;
- sharing a solution to a math problem with the group, recognizing an error, and asking others for assistance.

Third Grade

1 Demonstrates self-confidence.

Self-confidence grows through positive interactions with others and experiences of feeling competent. For most third graders, peers are an important source of validation and companionship. Students this age take pride in their accomplishments and can usually respect the accomplishments of their peers as well. Examples include:

- choosing work partners based on shared interests, such as writing adventure stories with someone who also likes this genre;
- seeking an alternate playmate when rejected by the first choice of a play partner;
- being able to move on after making a mistake;
- evaluating their own work and discussing it critically;
- acknowledging that someone else's strategy for solving a math problem is better than their own;
- complimenting or critiquing a peer's writing during a group sharing time;
- joining competitive games on the playground even though they often don't win.

I Personal and Social Development

A Self concept

Preschool-3	Preschool-4	Kindergarten

Preschool-3

2 Shows some self-direction.

Helping children make choices and perform tasks they are able to do fosters their independence. Some three year olds appear more independent than they really are because they frequently refuse to do things when they are asked. At this age, children can only make very simple choices (for example, between sand play and playing in the housekeeping area). They show their independence by:

- engaging eagerly in solitary or parallel play;
- washing hands before eating without an individual reminder;
- choosing specific materials for pasting from the collage collection;
- selecting one book from among several choices;
- hanging up their sweaters or coats after seeing others do it;
- observing and experimenting at the sand or water table;
- choosing one activity over another and participating in it.

Preschool-4

2 Shows some self-direction.

Four year olds often seem independent because they want to do everything on their own. However, they still require encouragement to act independently in unfamiliar situations or when trying challenging tasks. Four year olds can make simple choices among activities, but occasionally need support in trying new classroom activities. Examples of initiative and independence include:

- finding materials with which to work, such as scissors, tape, and markers, for acting on an idea or desire (for example, making a pretend camera for "taking pictures");
- finding and putting on one's own jacket, mittens, and hat before going outdoors;
- deciding to build an airport with blocks, forming a plan, and then implementing it with others already working with the blocks;
- trying a new activity (for example, soap painting or a cooking project), and pursuing it for a meaningful period of time;
- playing with different children rather than the same friend or friends every day;
- choosing one activity out of several and becoming involved with it.

Kindergarten

2 Shows initiative and self-direction.

Independence in thinking and action enables children to take responsibility for themselves. Most five year olds can make choices among familiar activities, participate in new experiences, and are willing to take some risks. Children who choose familiar activities repeatedly and are hesitant to venture into new areas need help from adults in order to expand their independence. Some examples of initiative and independence are:

- finding materials for projects (for example, glue to add their name card to a bar graph);
- eagerly selecting new activities during choice time, such as trying the carpentry table or the computer for the first time;
- assuming classroom chores without being asked (for example, sweeping sand from the floor, helping to clean up spilled juice);
- choosing to work on a social studies project because the activity interests them, rather than because friends are doing it;
- originating projects and working on them without extensive direction from the teacher.

First Grade

2 Shows initiative and self-direction.

Independence in thought and action is a sign of children's growing sense of personal responsibility. When provided with opportunities to do so, first graders want to make independent choices of materials, activities, and work/play partners. They can assume responsibility for routine tasks and carry them out with little or no assistance. Examples of how they demonstrate initiative and self-direction include:

- introducing a new idea for a game during recess;
- thinking up a project and getting started on it without extensive teacher direction;
- volunteering to help a friend who is having difficulty thinking of a story idea;
- helping with extra clean-up responsibilities in the classroom;
- transporting personal belongings to and from school (for example, homework, backpacks, notes to family members);
- deciding to work on something else during choice time because others have already selected their first choice.

Second Grade

2 Shows initiative and self-direction.

Independence in thinking and action is a sign of children's growing sense of personal responsibility. For second graders, initiative and self-direction include willingness to try new experiences, make independent choices, and assume independent responsibility for tasks. They demonstrate these skills by:

- willingly and independently taking on extra responsibilities in the classroom (for example, an extra clean-up task, setting up a display, or caring for the plants);
- assuming responsibility for personal needs (for example, readily finding a new reading book, bringing or wearing sneakers on gym days);
- appropriately declining help that is offered but not needed;
- trying to write poetry for the first time instead of producing another narrative during writing workshop;
- participating in a new classroom or recess activity;
- making a work plan and getting started on it (for example, deciding what to paint or which software to use).

Third Grade

2 Shows initiative and self-direction.

Most third graders have clear preferences and interests, often more closely aligned with those of peers than adults. For third graders, making good choices includes knowing how to generate options, weigh pros and cons, and recognize that attempting something new may be accompanied by initial discomfort. They demonstrate initiative and self-direction by:

- completing homework independently and bringing it to school on time;
- initiating independent projects (for example, learning how to play the recorder);
- evaluating the benefits and drawbacks of various ways to do a project before getting started;
- making work plans and getting started on them (choosing a role to play in a skit or a topic for a story);
- choosing and beginning to work on new activities without waiting for the teacher;
- discussing the pros and cons of a situation before making decisions.

I Personal and Social Development

B Self control

Preschool-3

1 Follows simple classroom rules and routines with guidance.

Three year olds function primarily within a world of their own making. They are only beginning to respond to simple rules and routines. They need many reminders and much support in learning the expectations of the classroom and appropriate behavior in preschool or child care. They show their emerging ability to follow rules and routines by:

- following simple classroom rules, such as "Do not hit other people," or telling the teacher when they have to use the bathroom;
- picking up their cups and napkins and putting them in the wastebasket after snack;
- keeping the sand inside the sand table after only a few reminders;
- showing a friend where to put unit blocks on the shelf during clean-up;
- standing in line at the slide while waiting for a turn to go up the steps.

Preschool-4

1 Follows simple classroom rules and routines.

Four year olds find established routines very comforting. They feel safer and better able to participate when rules are clear and followed consistently. They can follow simple rules and procedures with gentle reminders. They show their acceptance and understanding of rules and routines by:

- waiting patiently until someone leaves the water table when the rule is "only four people at a time";
- independently going to the circle area after clean-up;
- clearing off their places at the snack table by taking their cups to the designated place and throwing away their napkins and leftovers with few reminders;
- turning off the tape recorder after listening to a story;
- removing a finished painting from the easel and knowing where to hang it up to dry;
- holding hands when crossing a street that has no traffic light or crossing guard;
- washing hands before snack.

Kindergarten

1 Follows classroom rules and routines.

Children who are successful within a group know and accept the rules established for that particular group. Five year olds are learning this skill and can be quite stubborn with their peers, insisting on adherence to the rules. They are comfortable when they know the routines and can plan their activities around the daily schedule. Ways that children show this ability are:

- moving their name tags to the "In" column to show their attendance at school;
- remembering to wash hands before a cooking project;
- putting away a puzzle before starting another activity or shutting off the tape player before leaving the listening center;
- bringing a book with a torn page over to the book repair box;
- knowing that only three people can be at the computer at one time and writing their names on the waiting list to reserve a spot;
- recognizing that because it is almost time for snack, there is only enough time to build a small addition to their block structure.

First Grade

1 Follows classroom rules and routines.

Six year olds follow rules and routines best when they have helped shape them and when the rules are simple and consistent. They are beginning to understand and accept reasonable consequences for their behavior. Like five year olds, they can be stubborn with their peers, insisting on adherence to rules that even they sometimes forget. Some ways that six year olds demonstrate the ability to follow rules and routines are:

• arriving in the morning and knowing what to do to begin the day's activities;

• following the daily schedule without continually asking "What happens next?";

• locating and replacing personal belongings and classroom supplies;

• taking turns in group discussions;

• following the procedures for using the computer;

• cleaning up after work time and putting materials back in their proper place.

Second Grade

1 Follows classroom rules and routines.

Seven year olds follow rules and routines best when they have helped to shape them and when the rules remain consistent. They can understand and accept reasonable consequences for their behavior. Examples of following rules and routines include:

• locating and replacing personal belongings and classroom supplies independently;

• taking turns and listening respectfully to others in group discussions;

• finding a book and reading quietly during independent reading;

• proceeding quietly through the hallway when going from the classroom to the cafeteria;

• knowing the daily and weekly classroom schedule and routine (times for music, physical education, or writing workshop);

• speaking respectfully to others, even those with whom they disagree;

• assuming the role of "teacher of the day" and leading morning meeting effectively.

Third Grade

1 Acts with responsibility and independence.

Third graders are becoming more self-reliant. They can internalize school behaviors such as following rules and routines, managing transitions, and using materials carefully. They respond better to rules they help establish than to those imposed upon them, and they can accept reasonable consequences for their behavior. Some ways they demonstrate the ability to follow rules and routines are:

• locating necessary materials and quickly starting to work;

• reminding others of classroom rules and routines in supportive ways;

• knowing the daily and weekly schedule and following established routines;

• following the rules for group discussions (taking turns, listening to the ideas of others, sticking to a topic);

• using a CD-ROM in the media center and then returning it to the proper storage place when finished;

• entering or exiting the building, gym, or cafeteria quietly, whether alone or in a group;

• asking permission to use someone else's property and then returning it when finished.

Preschool-3

2 **Begins to use classroom materials carefully.**

At three years of age, children are just beginning to learn to take care of materials and put things back where they belong. They need modeling, guidance, and many reminders to do so. They show a developing sense of their responsibility by:

- taking care of books (for example, turning the pages carefully and putting books back on the shelf when finished);
- using magic markers on paper, rather than on other surfaces;
- putting caps back on markers when reminded to do so;
- putting toys away when finished, such as taking their puzzles back to the rack;
- treating classroom pets gently and with care.

Preschool-4

2 **Uses classroom materials carefully.**

In school, children are encouraged to take care of the materials they are using and keep the classroom in order. Four year olds are just beginning to take on this responsibility independently, although they need frequent reminders. Children show responsibility for materials by:

- helping to clean up by sweeping around the sand table;
- putting blocks away in designated places when the teacher announces it is clean-up time;
- looking at books carefully and putting them back on the shelf when finished;
- handling objects on the Discovery Table carefully;
- exploring the teacher's guitar gently, thoughtfully, and with care.

Kindergarten

2 **Uses classroom materials purposefully and respectfully.**

One of the major challenges of school for five year olds is learning how to care for classroom materials. With some reminders, a child learns how to use materials thoughtfully (so the materials continue to be available for others) and how to put things away so that others can easily find them. Examples include:

- hanging dress-up clothes on their proper hooks;
- asking for tape to repair a torn page in a book and sitting with the teacher while fixing it;
- using materials with intention, such as playing the piano with a song in mind, not just pounding;
- returning the disk to its box after working on the computer;
- using scissors appropriately for cutting and then putting them back in their assigned place;
- taking out the building blocks to create a structure rather than just emptying the shelves;
- using materials and equipment without breaking or destroying them.

First Grade

2 Uses materials purposefully and respectfully.

Six year olds are learning to care for the property of others. After they have received direction on how to use materials appropriately, it is reasonable to expect they can do so with only a few reminders. Examples include:

- using markers, crayons, and scissors, and then returning them to supply shelves or baskets when finished;
- locating a magnifier to look more closely at the butterfly's wings in order to add details to a drawing;
- borrowing colored pencils from another student and then returning them when finished;
- going to the math center to get the unifix cubes in order to solve a math problem;
- returning the computer disk to its proper location after finishing some work at the computer;
- washing paint brushes carefully before returning them to their container.

Second Grade

2 Uses materials purposefully and respectfully.

Learning responsible care and use of materials is an important aspect of maintaining a positive learning climate. Second graders can use materials independently and with intention, although they often need to review directions about how to do so. Examples include:

- finding software for the computer and returning it to the proper storage place when finished;
- setting up the paints and then cleaning up;
- locating and using appropriate materials with intention (getting a ruler to draw a straight line or using Cuisenaire rods to solve a math problem involving multiplication);
- assisting others with clean-up after putting away one's own work;
- asking a classmate for permission to use her or his belongings;
- storing adaptive equipment in places where it will not disrupt the flow of traffic (for example, placing crutches next to a chair when they are not in use).

Third Grade

See the following indicator on page 7 in Personal and Social Development:

A Self control
1 Acts with responsibility and independence.

❚❙ Personal and Social Development
B   Self control

Preschool-3

3 Manages transitions.

Children this age are beginning to learn how to accept change without undue distress. Although they may be uncomfortable with the major transition from home to school, they can learn simple classroom transition routines and begin to show comfort with small changes. They show the ability to manage transitions by:

- separating from a parent (or caregiver) at the door with growing ease;
- moving from one classroom activity to the next with a few reminders;
- cleaning up and coming to the snack table after only a few reminders;
- after initially protesting, giving a truck or other toy to another child who has been waiting for a turn;
- responding positively to the signal for a change in activity;
- hanging up their sweaters or jackets upon arrival and joining the classroom activity;
- saying good-bye to the teacher as they go out the door at the end of the day.

Preschool-4

3 Manages transitions.

Four year olds sometimes are upset when routines change or things are done differently. They manage transitions most successfully when they are told what to expect in advance. Children show they are learning to manage transitions by:

- using a routine, such as waving from the window or blowing a kiss goodbye, to manage the transition from home to school;
- accepting transitions with little or no protest;
- moving from free play to clean-up with ease and purposefulness;
- helping the teacher give transition signals;
- cleaning up ahead of schedule because a visitor has come to lead a special group time.

Kindergarten

3 Manages transitions and adapts to changes in routine.

Adapting to and accepting changes in routine is an important skill if children are to function comfortably in school. Five year olds are anxious to establish order in their lives and prefer consistent routines. However, because change is also a part of growth, children need to acquire flexibility in order to deal with change. Five year olds are beginning to adjust to changes and learn that different situations call for different behaviors. Children show this flexibility by:

- going from home to school without anxiety;
- moving smoothly from one routine to another (for example, from activity period to clean-up, or from story time to getting ready to go home);
- remembering to whisper when visiting the library;
- going to music class and following the music teacher's rules about where to sit;
- greeting visitors who come into the classroom and then continuing with their work;
- anticipating the afternoon assembly with pleasure, even though it means they will miss gym class.

First Grade

3 Manages transitions and adapts to new places and events.

Adapting to or accepting changes in routine are important skills for children to acquire. Most first graders enjoy and rely on classroom routines and clearly defined procedures for transitions. With advance preparation, six year olds can adjust to changes in routines (for example, a change in schedule, a substitute teacher) or new situations and can adapt their behavior accordingly. Examples of their growing skills include:

- moving from one activity to another with minimal teacher guidance (for example, putting away quiet reading books and lining up for music);

- leaving a task unfinished to be completed at another time (for example, setting their journals aside and returning to them after lunch);

- going to music class and following the music teacher's rules about where to sit and how to behave;

- asking about a change on the daily schedule posted in the classroom;

- accepting that gym time has been canceled and that classroom game time will replace it.

Second Grade

3 Manages transitions and adapts to new places and events.

Second graders rely on the predictability and consistency of routines and transitions. An unannounced or sudden change (for example, a substitute teacher or the cancellation of an activity) may cause them to feel uncertain or anxious; but given a little time and support, they can adjust. They demonstrate transition skills by:

- moving from one activity to another with minimal teacher guidance (such as coming in from outdoor recess and settling down for quiet reading);

- stopping a woodworking project because choice time is over, but accepting that the project can be completed the next day;

- accepting with little difficulty changes in routine when the teacher is absent and a substitute teacher is present;

- checking the posted daily schedule regularly upon arrival and noticing when a change occurs;

- adjusting to a change in the classroom schedule and moving into new or unplanned activities with relative ease.

Third Grade

2 Uses coping strategies to manage a range of feelings and situations.

Third graders are learning how to manage the range of emotions and feelings that come with growing up, making and keeping friends, accepting change, and handling increasingly difficult school work. With adult support, they can begin to use coping strategies, such as talking over problems with a peer or adult or taking time out from frustrating activities, then returning to them with a new perspective. Some examples include:

- responding to the teacher's request to put things away and get ready to work on math, even though they are disappointed that they have to stop what they are doing;

- being left out of a game and finding some other children with whom to play;

- feeling frustrated about a change in the schedule and talking with the teacher about a way to deal with their disappointment;

- taking a break before trying to complete a frustrating task;

- getting angry about losing a game and then talking it over with a friend to calm down;

- discussing their own and others' feelings openly.

▌I▐ Personal and Social Development
C   Approaches to learning

Preschool-3	**Preschool-4**	**Kindergarten**

1 Shows eagerness and curiosity as a learner.

Preschool-3

Three year olds are naturally curious about everything in their world and are beginning to respond to what they observe. Examples of this curiosity include:

- checking the gerbil cage daily to see where the gerbil is hiding;
- trying different art experiences and puzzles, or listening to new books;
- indicating awareness of other children by watching or interacting with them;
- noticing new displays in the science area and talking about them with a teacher;
- showing interest in many different classroom activities.

Preschool-4

Most four year olds are naturally curious and continually ask questions about everything they encounter. They display growing maturity when they respond to answers to their questions by asking for clarification or additional information, rather than saying "Why? Why?" Examples include:

- showing interest in stories and events related by other children;
- being excited and curious about new things in the classroom, such as a collection of fall leaves or shells from the sea shore;
- looking at a picture of a castle and trying to reproduce it with blocks;
- continuing a discussion by asking related questions or making comments;
- asking how water makes the wheel turn at the water table.

Kindergarten

Five year olds are curious, active learners, excited about their environment and the wide variety of materials available to them in school. They enjoy using realistic props in dramatic play and experimenting with different artistic media. They are fascinated by audiovisual media and by technology and can become very insistent when they have strong ideas about what they want to do. Examples include:

- showing interest in and asking questions about stories and events related by other children;
- using play and a variety of different media to process new ideas and represent knowledge;
- demonstrating the meaning of "sinking" and "floating" by acting out how the rubber duck floats and the paper clip sinks;
- asking how the caterpillar can live in the cocoon with no food or water;
- using a computerized painting program to depict their houses and yards;
- acting out how angry their own mother was when the car broke down while telling the story to the teacher.

First Grade

1 Shows eagerness and curiosity as a learner.

Because six year olds learn from direct experience, they are most likely to show interest and curiosity in learning experiences in which they have an active role. They demonstrate interest and curiosity in different ways, depending on their individual learning styles and previous experiences. Some children express themselves through art, construction, music, or dramatics, while others use words or actions. Examples include:

- bringing in a book from home about a topic being discussed in school;
- contributing an anecdote to a class discussion based on something learned earlier;
- making puppets based on a story read by the teacher and carefully working to capture the details of each character;
- seeking more specific information about a subject (for example, looking in the class library for books about insects after going on a science walk to collect small creatures);
- demonstrating knowledge and interest about a specific topic (for example, by drawing detailed pictures and reading books about bats).

Second Grade

1 Shows eagerness and curiosity as a learner.

Seven year olds continue to learn primarily through direct, active experience and are beginning to understand and express abstract ideas through pictures, words, and symbolic forms. They demonstrate interest and curiosity as learners in different ways, depending on their own learning styles and previous experiences. Some children express themselves primarily through art, construction, music, movement, or dramatics, while others use mostly verbal and written language. Examples include:

- seeking additional information about topics of study (for example, getting books from the library to learn more about rain forests);
- pursuing an independent project with intensity, such as building a model of a suspension bridge after hearing about one in a story;
- reading several books by the same author and then attempting to use the author's style in their own writing;
- thinking up a new verse to a favorite class song;
- returning to the science table every day to weigh classroom objects and keep track of their weights.

Third Grade

1 Shows eagerness and curiosity as a learner.

Third graders are developing the ability to express and understand abstract ideas through pictures, words, and symbolic forms. Because students demonstrate interest and curiosity as learners in different ways, it is important to provide them with many means of expression. Some children express themselves through art, construction, music, movement, or dramatics, while others use predominantly verbal and written language. Examples include:

- exploring a special interest in some depth (for example, reading a series of biographies about famous sports figures or building an elaborate project about birds in the rain forest);
- bringing in an article about a local environmental issue and following up on it in some way (suggesting a class project, such as writing letters to local officials);
- using the Internet to learn more about a topic being studied by the class;
- recalling information from a family experience and applying it to a classroom activity;
- asking probing questions while on a field trip and taking notes on the responses.

Preschool-3

2 Attends briefly, and seeks help when encountering a problem.

At three, children can attend to activities or stories for brief periods of time (5–10 minutes). They will stay involved longer if the activity is a favorite one. However, if they encounter a problem, they usually wander away from the activity rather than continuing to try to solve the problem. They require very specific help in problem-solving and explicit physical guidance when following suggestions. They show increasing ability to attend and persist by:

- listening to a story with a small group of children;
- seeking assistance after trying for a minute or two to put together a difficult puzzle;
- trying several times to reach a toy on a high shelf before giving up;
- looking for help when trying to hang up a painting that is still wet;
- following the teacher's suggestion when unable to choose an activity or when too many children select the same activity area.

Preschool-4

2 Attends to tasks and seeks help when encountering a problem.

Four year olds attend to most tasks for short periods of time (10–20 minutes). They will persist longer when they have chosen the activity. Learning to work until tasks are finished or problems are solved is often difficult for this age group. Ways that children show persistence and willingness to accept help in problem-solving include:

- paying attention to songs and stories during circle time;
- raising their hands or touching the teacher's arm to indicate that they need help;
- trying to start the zippers on their coats repeatedly until they can do the task without help;
- following teacher or peer suggestions for solving a problem (for example, understanding that putting another block at the base of the tower would make it more stable);
- completing favorite puzzles over and over again;
- beginning to put the blocks away and asking for help to finish more quickly;
- accepting help from the teacher when putting together a difficult puzzle.

Kindergarten

2 Sustains attention to a task, persisting even after encountering difficulty.

Five year olds can attend to open-ended tasks they have chosen for reasonably long periods of time (20–30 minutes). However, it is more difficult for them to concentrate on tasks they have not selected or activities that require skills beyond their current abilities. When engaged in challenging tasks, they may need encouragement to continue. They are beginning to understand that making mistakes is an important part of learning and acquiring new skills. Some examples include:

- watching the new class gerbil eat and play on the wheel in the cage for most of choice time;
- making several attempts at solving a problem (for example, trying different ways to attach tape when building a 3-D collage);
- continuing projects from one day to the next, such as working on a clay sculpture for several days or creating pictures for a storybook;
- counting the blocks with the teacher as she helps rearrange them to make it easier for the big truck to park in the block garage.

First Grade

2 Sustains attention to work over a period of time.

Six year olds can attend to interesting tasks they have chosen for extended periods of time (30 minutes or longer). As they work on engaging projects and activities, they begin to understand that their work can not always be finished in one sitting, but can be completed at a later time. They are also learning that mistakes are part of learning and growing. Examples include:

- drawing a detailed picture of the characters from a story and staying focused until the picture is completed;
- choosing to work on a jigsaw puzzle for several days in a row;
- extending work on a project over the course of several days (for example, constructing a boat, returning to it the next day and making a sea, and then adding fish to the sea on the third day);
- working diligently to master a computer game;
- putting away a story and returning to work on it the next day;
- returning repeatedly to the math center to work with tangrams in an effort to solve the problem of making a square.

Second Grade

2 Sustains attention to work over a period of time.

Seven year olds are able to concentrate for extended periods of time (30 minutes or more) in order to complete the projects they begin. They strive for perfection and often need support to understand that accomplishment comes with practice and a number of failures. Examples include:

- running out of time when constructing an intricate pattern block design, yet returning the next day to recreate the design and add to it;
- staying with a chapter book until it is completed;
- using the computer to write a story over a period of several days;
- working with persistence and patience on a group project (for example, a painted mural of the desert);
- making several attempts to solve a math problem, but not giving up before arriving at the correct answer;
- running out of time at recess before a soccer game is over and returning to finish it the next day.

Third Grade

2 Begins to use time constructively and works in a focused manner.

Many third graders are self-motivated and can concentrate on projects of interest for extended periods of time (40 minutes or longer). Their desire to finish their work can sometimes lead to rushing through things. Finding ways to raise their level of personal investment in projects diminishes this tendency. Examples of how third graders show their ability to sustain interest include:

- working on a challenging set of math problems for several days in a row;
- making a diorama for a book report that requires work outside of school;
- taking on and completing a multi-step computer project over the course of several work periods;
- reading a number of books by the same author;
- spending several weeks working on an elaborate social studies project;
- memorizing their lines in a play over the course of several rehearsals;
- working on a poem over several days.

Preschool-3

3 Approaches play with purpose and inventiveness.

Three year olds are just beginning to learn how to use materials as they are meant to be used. Play is mainly exploratory, helping children learn about the properties and characteristics of materials and equipment. At this time, three year olds show emerging flexibility and inventiveness by:

- taking play dough to the housekeeping area to fill the muffin tins before putting them in the play oven;
- getting the snap-it beads from the manipulative shelf to make a necklace for dress-up;
- becoming excited when yellow and blue paint turn into green after being mixed;
- suggesting that they feed the leftover carrot scrapings from a cooking project to the rabbit;
- trying a different way to accomplish a task or use an object.

Preschool-4

3 Approaches tasks with flexibility and inventiveness.

Four year olds, who are most comfortable with repetition and familiar people and places, often do not understand that there are different ways to work with materials or to solve problems. They are just beginning to understand that there are many possible ways to accomplish a task. Children show flexibility and willingness to try new ideas by:

- using two short cardboard tubes as binoculars in the dramatic play area;
- trying to staple pieces of paper together after unsuccessfully trying to tape them together;
- trying several different ways to form play dough into a specific object such as a birthday cake or snowman;
- using prior experience to figure out what to do in present situations (for example, asking the teacher for red paint to color the play dough because last week the teacher made the play dough green with green paint);
- experimenting with a brush to find ways to keep paint from dripping;
- implementing the suggestions of others (for example, playing a different role than usual during dramatic play).

Kindergarten

3 Approaches tasks with flexibility and inventiveness.

Five year olds are learning how to approach tasks creatively and to attempt more than one way to solve a problem. Trial and error nurtures and encourages their creativity. Some children are reluctant to try new approaches because an unsuccessful outcome may be difficult to accept. After children have tried repeatedly to solve problems, it is important for them to know when and where to get help before they become frustrated. Examples include:

- creating something new (for example, a pretend camera) by combining several familiar materials (for example, a milk carton and tape);
- asking for and accepting suggestions for alternate ways to build a tall tower that will remain standing;
- using table blocks and small vehicles and figures to explain to a friend how they get to school;
- communicating frustration in an acceptable way after failing to accomplish a task;
- using a drawing program on the computer to illustrate a story;
- using resources to spell words needed to write a sign.

First Grade

3 Approaches tasks with flexibility and inventiveness.

First graders who are flexible and inventive can tackle problems with an open mind, try different approaches, and seek help when they reach an obstacle. Their inventiveness is often expressed through imaginative play. Examples of first graders demonstrating their flexibility and inventiveness include:

- creating a new ending to a story and acting it out;
- coming up with a creative way to make a home for a hermit crab;
- making up a new verse to a favorite class song;
- using materials in new ways (using unifix cubes as weight units on a balance scale);
- inventing a math game using dice or playing cards;
- seeing themselves as problem solvers (for example, while working on a difficult project, calling out to others, "Hey! I've got a great idea.");
- mixing paint to create a greater variety of colors.

Second Grade

3 Approaches tasks with flexibility and inventiveness.

Flexible thinkers in a second grade classroom tackle problems with open minds, try different approaches, consider alternative ideas, and know when to seek help. Examples include:

- finding a way to pursue a personal interest (for example, animals) within the boundaries of whatever activity they might choose (selecting books about animals or writing a story and drawing pictures of animals);
- using alternative materials or equipment if a first choice does not work or is unavailable;
- thinking of a creative way to make scenery for a skit or puppet show;
- considering different ways to measure classroom dimensions (using lengths of string, a trundle wheel, or Cuisenaire rods);
- working with one or two others to invent a new game or create a variation on an existing game;
- using materials from the art area to help with a science investigation.

Third Grade

3 Approaches tasks with flexibility and inventiveness.

Flexible and inventive third graders tackle problems with open minds, try different approaches, consider alternative ideas, and know when to seek help. Examples include:

- considering alternative approaches before getting started (pondering a few choices for a story before beginning to write);
- using alternate materials or equipment if a first choice does not work or is unavailable;
- experimenting with new methods for estimating and counting (for example, instead of counting by tens, deciding to count by twenties);
- presenting a problem to the class in order to hear other solutions and then selecting one to try (for example, sharing several possible scenarios in order to come up with an ending to a story);
- suggesting a solution to a class problem being discussed by the whole group.

I Personal and Social Development

C Approaches to learning

Preschool-3	**Preschool-4**	**Kindergarten**

Preschool-3

Not expected at this level.

Preschool-4

Not expected at this level.

Kindergarten

See the following indicator on page 16 in Personal and Social Development:

C Approaches to learning

3 Approaches tasks with flexibility and inventiveness.

See the following indicator on page 100 in Mathematical Thinking:

E Measurement

2 Explores common instruments for measuring during work and play.

See the following indicator on page 114 in Scientific Thinking:

A Inquiry

2 Uses simple tools and equipment to extend the senses and gather data.

See the following indicator on page 142 in Social Studies:

B Human interdependence

3 Begins to be aware of technology and how it affects life.

First Grade

4 **Begins to use technology to assist with thinking and problem-solving.**

When children receive instruction and have opportunities to use computers and other forms of technology in the classroom, they develop an appreciation for how these tools can help them learn. First graders are beginning to understand how to use basic computer hardware and software as well as other electronic equipment (for example, VCRs, audiotape players, cameras). Some examples include:

- publishing a story using a computer;
- operating the VCR controls for a small group watching a nature video;
- asking for the teacher's help to get information about Alaska from the Internet;
- using a drawing program to create a picture to accompany a story;
- knowing the correct buttons to use to control the audiotape player (rewind, fast forward, pause, stop, play);
- asking the teacher for permission to use the class camera to take a photograph of an elaborate pattern block design.

Second Grade

4 **Uses technology to assist with thinking and problem-solving.**

When children receive instruction and have opportunities to use computers and other forms of technology in the classroom, they develop an appreciation for how these tools can help them learn. Second graders can be expected to understand how to use basic computer hardware and software, as well as other electronic equipment (for example, VCRs, audiotape players, cameras). Some examples of technology skills include:

- publishing a story using a computer;
- using the Internet to get more information about a topic of interest;
- using a digital camera to create illustrations for a story;
- sending an e-mail to a friend who moved away;
- pressing the appropriate buttons on the TV and VCR so the setup works correctly;
- knowing how to rewind a video or audio tape, stop it, then review it for clarification;
- using a CD player to provide background music for a skit.

Third Grade

4 **Uses technology to assist with thinking and problem-solving.**

When children receive instruction and have opportunities to use different forms of technology in the classroom, they develop an appreciation for how these tools help them learn. Third graders should be able to use computer hardware and software, as well as other electronic equipment (for example, VCRs, audiotape players, digital cameras). Some examples of their skills in this area include:

- sending an e-mail message to an expert to learn more about a topic being discussed in school;
- using CD-ROMs to gather information for a research project;
- accessing the Internet to get more information about a topic of interest;
- creating charts and graphs on the computer;
- adding photographs taken with a digital camera to a final project;
- using an audiotape player to create a sound track for a skit or puppet show.

Preschool-3

1 Interacts with one or more children.

At three, children are just beginning to learn social skills and how to interact with peers. They still need considerable support and practice. Their play is usually parallel (side-by-side), with only brief interactions with other children. Children show their emerging social skills by:

- participating in classroom routines, such as helping classmates sweep up sand around the sand table, or joining other children feeding the fish;
- playing side-by-side with other children in the dramatic play area, occasionally making comments to a nearby child;
- helping another child set the table for snack;
- participating with other children at the play dough table;
- talking with others during snack or lunch.

Preschool-4

1 Interacts easily with one or more children.

At age four, preschoolers are beginning to make the transition from parallel play to cooperative play. Taking turns, sharing, and conversing during play are new skills for many four year olds. They are developing special friendships and starting to understand that it is possible to have more than one friend at a time. Examples of interaction skills include:

- playing with whomever is in the dramatic play area rather than only playing there when alone or with a special friend;
- making decisions with another child about who will put out the cups and napkins and how many they will need;
- working cooperatively with another child who is painting on the same side of the easel;
- removing the toys from the sand table with a friend in order to start a new project;
- talking (or using alternative communication) with another child to plan ways to build a block structure;
- using rhythm instruments with several children.

Kindergarten

1 Interacts easily with one or more children.

Five year old children are beginning to play cooperatively with one or more children, listen to peers and understand their feelings, and solve problems cooperatively. The meaning of friendship (What does having a friend mean? How does friendship work?) is very interesting to them. They have preferences about who they want to play with and are sometimes tentative about interacting with peers they do not know very well. Examples include:

- playing cooperatively with a group of children during recess;
- following suggestions given by a friend about how to proceed in their play (for example, deciding to build a fire station with the large hollow blocks in response to a friend's suggestion);
- asking a friend politely to borrow the scissors and saying "thank you" when returning them;
- choosing to work with children who are new to the class;
- giving assistance to peers who are trying to solve a problem (helping to tie shoes or figuring out how to divide the Legos among three children).

First Grade

1 **Interacts easily with peers.**

Knowing how to relate positively to peers and how to make friends is essential to children's sense of competence. Making friends and having a best friend are important to most first graders. They are eager to socialize with peers and often have strong preferences about those with whom they want to work and play. Examples include:

- readily sitting with a group of children at the lunch or snack table;
- giving and receiving peer assistance during work times (for example, helping someone figure out how to spell a word);
- showing appreciation of other children by smiling, asking questions, or making positive comments during group time;
- suggesting that someone join a group in order to share the markers;
- participating comfortably with a small group of children working on a skit;
- working cooperatively with several children on a math task.

Second Grade

1 **Interacts easily with peers.**

Knowing how to relate positively to peers and make friends is essential to a child's sense of competence. When second graders initiate the activity or select their partners, most can work, play, and interact cooperatively and successfully. Examples of how seven year olds demonstrate their ability to interact cooperatively include:

- giving and receiving assistance on a group project (for example, building a model, making a terrarium);
- playing a computer game with two friends;
- letting others join games that are already underway;
- working cooperatively on a small group project (a book group, research task, or graphing project) initiated by a teacher;
- playing tag with several children during recess;
- initiating conversation with a new student and showing her/him around the school.

Third Grade

1 **Interacts easily with peers.**

Knowing how to make friends and relate positively to peers is essential to a child's overall sense of competence. Developing and maintaining close friendships is very important to third graders. Trying to understand where they fit into the social fabric of the group demands a great deal of their energy. Some ways that third graders show they can interact easily and cooperatively include:

- playing with a best friend at choice time or recess and letting a third person join in;
- considering how to change an activity so a physically-challenged classmate can participate;
- cooperating in groups or pairs on teacher-initiated tasks (for example, working on math problems, creating skits and puppet shows, or completing a social studies research report);
- welcoming a new player into a game that has begun already;
- assuming both leader and follower roles in group activities;
- working with students from another class on a dramatic production.

I Personal and Social Development

D Interaction with others

Preschool-3

2 Interacts with familiar adults.

Three year olds vary greatly in how they relate to adults. Some are comfortable and interact spontaneously, while other children need time to warm up, become comfortable, or feel safe with adults. Children show increasing comfort by:

- entering the classroom in the morning with a greeting for the teacher;
- responding to questions the teacher asks;
- running over to the adult who is bringing in lunch and asking if they can help;
- sharing the latest classroom news with the school secretary or custodian;
- communicating with the teacher or other adult about the new dress or shirt they are wearing;
- telling an adult about an event happening at home, such as, "Today is my brother's birthday."

Preschool-4

2 Interacts easily with familiar adults.

Four year olds are learning how to interact with adults. They engage in conversations and follow directions given by familiar adults much more readily than with unfamiliar adults. Some children need explicit instruction about positive ways to say "hello," respond to adults' comments and questions, or gain an adult's attention. Children show their skills in this area by:

- responding appropriately when an adult says, "Good morning";
- answering a teacher's question about who they played with on the playground;
- asking for attention by raising a hand, touching the teacher's arm, or other reasonable actions;
- listening to and talking with adults.

Kindergarten

2 Interacts easily with familiar adults.

Young children often have more experience talking and interacting with adults than with their peers. Five year olds who feel at ease with adults will show affection, respond to questions, initiate conversations, and follow directions given by familiar adults. Examples include:

- greeting the teacher or other adults when arriving in the morning;
- expressing curiosity about a new adult in the classroom by asking questions about who he is or why he is there;
- relating events and anecdotes to the teacher with ease and comfort;
- following directions given by a parent volunteer about when to get off the bus during a field trip;
- interacting easily with other adults in the school, such as the custodian, the lunch room monitor, or the crossing guard.

First Grade

2 Interacts easily with adults.

At six, children are working toward greater independence from adults, but they want adults close by for approval and support. First graders who are at ease with adults will respond to questions, initiate conversations, and seek their assistance. They demonstrate skills in this area by:

- telling the teacher about yesterday's family outing;
- taking directions from and conversing with a parent chaperone on a field trip to the apple orchard;
- greeting visitors to the class and showing them around;
- responding positively to the teacher aide on the playground;
- participating in informal conversations with adults during snack time or lunch;
- responding appropriately to greetings from teachers or other adults when arriving in the morning;
- asking a question of the museum docent during a field trip.

Second Grade

2 Interacts easily with adults.

By seven, children express the desire to be independent of adults; however, they want adults close by for approval and support. Examples of how seven year olds show their comfort with adults are:

- discussing a personal problem with the classroom teacher, a resource teacher, or a classroom volunteer;
- responding appropriately to greetings from teachers or other adults when arriving in the morning;
- talking about a story with a teacher and getting some ideas about possible endings;
- bringing a teacher's note to the office and talking comfortably with the school secretary;
- chatting with a museum guide about an exhibit on a class trip;
- sharing a detailed drawing of a spider with the teacher and asking for feedback.

Third Grade

2 Interacts easily with adults.

Eight year olds are becoming increasingly independent from adults. They enjoy interactions with adults when they do not feel overly controlled by them. Examples of ways they demonstrate comfortable interactions with adults are:

- inviting the teacher to be the fourth player in a board game;
- solving problems with the help of the teacher, an assistant, or the parent of a friend;
- asking the teacher to make a book recommendation;
- volunteering to help the teacher with organizational tasks (for example, stapling, collating, or preparing materials for a project);
- responding appropriately to greetings from teachers or other adults;
- greeting the cafeteria servers by name at lunch time.

Preschool-3

3 Participates in the group life of the class.

Three year olds are very egocentric. Functioning as a group member and accommodating group expectations are difficult for many three year olds; they need guidance from the teacher to learn these things and adjust to being in school. At this age, children enjoy participating in simple action games that involve minimal time spent waiting for a turn. They show this growing awareness of the group life of the class by:

- participating in small group projects for 5-10 minutes, such as helping to fill the water table;
- noticing who is absent from circle time;
- paying attention to the class signals for clean-up or for listening to the teacher;
- bringing a favorite toy from home to share with the class;
- playing group games, such as Duck-Duck-Goose or Follow the Leader, with adult help;
- participating in snack time with peers, learning how to pour juice, how many crackers to take, and how to clean up when finished;
- joining a small group for a walk around the block.

Preschool-4

3 Participates in the group life of the class.

Children this age are beginning to show appreciation of group experiences and awareness of group expectations. However, they often need to be reminded of rules and routines. It is easier for them if group rules, such as how many children can play at the water table, are discussed with them in advance and if they have a part in establishing expectations. Four year olds are just beginning to play simple board and card games with rules. They show a growing ability to participate in the group life of the class by:

- readily joining circle times, participating in clean-up time, and going to snack when it is ready;
- noticing that a friend needs help putting away the blocks and going over to help, even though they had not played in the block area;
- recognizing that a classmate is absent and asking the teacher about it;
- suggesting silly and funny ideas for open-ended songs such as "Aiken Drum" or suggesting the animals for choruses of "Old MacDonald Had a Farm";
- playing simple Lotto games or board games, such as Candy Land.

Kindergarten

3 Participates in the group life of the class.

Five year olds show a sense of community by contributing ideas, taking responsibility for events in the classroom, sharing knowledge of classroom routines and procedures, and following rules in group games and activities. They can usually follow group expectations, especially if they have had previous school experience. Five year olds show their understanding of group life by:

- taking part in group activities, such as circle, music, or story time;
- being part of the audience as well as an active participant in group events;
- pitching in to clean up the block area, even though they didn't work there today;
- following the rules for simple card games (Go Fish or Concentration) and guessing games (I Spy);
- hunting through toy containers to find the lost marker caps;
- offering to show a new classmate where they hang up coats;
- waiting for turns.

First Grade

3 Participates in the group life of the class.

Six year olds are developing a sense of responsibility to others and beginning to understand how groups function and why groups need rules. They are learning to take turns, share, listen to others, and play games with rules. Although they voice concerns about fairness, they often want to be first, expect to win, and adjust the rules to meet their needs. Examples of how six year olds demonstrate the ability to participate in groups are:

- listening and participating at a school assembly;
- listening to classmates' ideas during group discussions;
- making contributions to group efforts, such as making props for a class play;
- waiting for their turns in games that involve the whole class (games like "I am thinking of a number");
- taking turns fairly in games played by several players;
- participating in games with rules that involve winning and losing with one or two other players (for example, bingo, Connect Four, checkers).

Second Grade

3 Participates in the group life of the class.

Seven year olds are learning how to work in groups and how groups function. Through classroom meetings and cooperative group work, they develop respect and responsibility for the community. Group life is becoming increasingly important to them as they identify more closely with peers. Ways they demonstrate skills in this area are:

- participating willingly as an active player or audience member in group events (for example, in class games, or at assemblies);
- considering the ideas of others when making group plans (constructing pulleys during a science activity or creating a class newspaper);
- helping others complete classroom jobs after they finish their own, so that everything is ready by day's end;
- going along with the rest of the group when playing a game, even when the group's ideas differ from their own;
- helping a group get organized for a playground game (soccer, kickball, jump rope) and then participating in it.

Third Grade

3 Participates in the group life of the class and school.

Through classroom discussions and cooperative group work, third graders develop respect and responsibility for the community that extends beyond their classrooms. Playing fairly and cooperatively for third graders includes adhering to the rules, taking turns, and watching the actions of others, even when it's not one's turn. Some examples are:

- making contributions to group efforts (a class bake sale, a recycling project) and assuming different roles as leader or follower;
- considering the ideas of others when making group plans;
- representing the class on an all-school committee;
- going along with the rest of the group when playing, even if the group's decision differs from their own (for example, accepting a judgment about whether a ball was actually out of bounds during a basketball game);
- volunteering to help with a class clean-up, even when they are not directly responsible for the clutter.

Preschool-3

4 Shows empathy and caring for others.

Even at three years of age, children show caring for those around them. Empathy is elicited by concrete occurrences that are similar to the child's experiences. For example, three year olds can sympathize with a child who has fallen down or who can't get his coat on. Children show their caring by:

- putting an arm around a friend who is crying;
- pretending to soothe a crying baby in the house area;
- asking an adult to help when a friend has trouble pulling on boots;
- being concerned when a friend falls and scrapes a knee;
- watching curiously when another child enters the classroom crying;
- helping a classmate clean up a spill.

Preschool-4

4 Shows empathy and caring for others.

At four years of age, many children show that they are aware of the feelings of their classmates. Other four year olds need to be taught to notice their peers and to understand the emotions and experiences of others. Children this age are generally better able to show caring for real people or book characters than abstract ideas or situations. Examples of caring behavior include:

- volunteering to sit next to a new child and helping the child with the procedures for snack;
- expressing sadness to a friend whose pet has died;
- going over to a friend who has fallen and giving comfort;
- expressing appropriate feelings (joy, sadness, fear) for characters in a story;
- getting help for classmates who cannot get their boots on or cannot find their paintings to take home;
- showing acceptance and support of a classmate with a physical disability.

Kindergarten

4 Shows empathy and caring for others.

Learning to recognize the feelings of others is an important life skill. Although some children express care and understanding for others' feelings almost naturally, other children need guidance and support from teachers to acquire these skills. Examples include:

- helping a friend find a lost toy;
- being concerned and wanting to help when a classmate falls and hurts her/himself;
- trying to help when a classmate's block structure has fallen;
- showing a new student around the room and telling her about center activities, rules and routines;
- sharing a friend's excitement about going to a baseball game;
- showing concern for a friend who has been excluded from a game or dramatic play;
- carrying something for a child who is using crutches;
- displaying concern about a friend's sister who is in the hospital.

First Grade

4 Shows empathy and caring for others.

Learning to appreciate the concerns of others is an important life skill. Some children show caring and empathy for others easily, while others need adult and peer guidance to acquire these qualities. Many six year olds are still somewhat egocentric, so they are inconsistent about considering the viewpoints of others. Examples of how six year olds show empathy and caring include:

- staying inside at recess to keep a sick friend company;
- helping a peer rebuild a Lego structure that was knocked down;
- deciding to leave a game and play with a friend when the friend is unable to join the game;
- offering to assist a child with a disability who cannot reach something on an upper shelf;
- expressing concern for a child whose pet just died;
- helping a newcomer to the class get settled into routines;
- complimenting the work of others and offering constructive suggestions when asked.

Second Grade

4 Shows empathy and caring for others.

Learning to appreciate the concerns of others is an important life skill. Seven year olds are learning to consider others' viewpoints. Some children this age naturally show caring and empathy while others need guidance and support from adults and peers to acquire these qualities. Examples include:

- helping a peer with a difficult assignment, even if it means missing the opportunity to do something new;
- staying inside at recess to keep an injured friend company;
- including less popular peers in group activities;
- responding to the teacher's news that a classmate's grandparent has died by suggesting that the class make cards to send to the family;
- recognizing and accepting the strengths and weaknesses of a friend;
- expressing concern for someone experiencing a problem (for example, saying to a friend, "Your cat died? You must feel awful!");
- informing the teacher that a classmate needs some assistance.

Third Grade

4 Shows empathy and caring for others.

Learning to appreciate the concerns of others is an important life skill. Eight year olds can be sensitive to the feelings of others and consider another person's point of view. Examples of how eight year olds show empathy and caring include:

- expressing concern for peers experiencing problems (an accident, a death in the family, a fire at home);
- expressing concern and interest about a community problem (homelessness, pollution) through comments made during group discussions;
- writing an apology note to someone they have hurt or offended;
- considering the needs of a classmate with a disability (for example, holding a door open for a classmate in a wheelchair or remembering to face a hearing-impaired classmate when speaking);
- finding a way to include less popular peers in group activities;
- helping younger children on the playground.

I Personal and Social Development
E Social problem-solving

Preschool-3

1 Seeks adult help when needed to resolve conflicts.

Three year olds do not have the skills to settle conflicts on their own. They learn to solve conflicts gradually by watching a teacher model effective conflict resolution strategies and by experiencing compromises facilitated by teachers or other adults. At this age, the expectation is that children will begin to recognize when they need some help to solve a problem. Examples include:

- seeking assistance when disturbed by a child who paints on their pictures or knocks down a block structure;
- asking for help when a child grabs a truck or other plaything;
- seeking help when another child is hitting or pushing;
- yelling at another child, "You can't come in the house area—it's full," and then calling the teacher for help;
- asking for help to get a ride on the Big Wheel or a turn on the slide.

Preschool-4

1 Seeks adult help when needed to resolve conflicts.

Four year olds need a great deal of adult support and guidance in learning how to settle conflicts (for example, how to share a limited amount of materials or deciding who will get to go outside first). Their natural responses are physical, such as hitting, kicking, or throwing. They are beginning to learn alternatives from adults who suggest and model ways to use words and other simple formulas. Children show they are gaining awareness of alternatives by:

- asking an adult to help when another child wants the same truck or when other children keep pushing in the line waiting for a turn on the slide;
- using words suggested by an adult to express anger, such as, "I don't like it when you push me" or "That makes me mad!";
- asking a child to return a toy he or she has grabbed, and turning to an adult for help when the child refuses;
- giving alternatives to friends, such as, "I'm playing with these, you play with those";
- asking the teacher to use a timer to decide when one child's turn on the bike ends and their own turn begins.

Kindergarten

1 Seeks adult help and begins to use simple strategies to resolve conflicts.

An initial step in conflict resolution is recognizing when there is a conflict and getting help to solve it. Communicating and using varied strategies to resolve conflicts (for example, "fair trades" or taking turns by mutual agreement) are emerging skills for five year olds. They still need adult support and modeling to use words to solve problems, suggest possible solutions, and participate in compromise. Children show they are learning these skills by:

- asking for help when a second child wants to use the same blocks;
- asking the teacher to set the timer so each person will know how long he or she can use the computer;
- negotiating with another child to divide the markers and determine how many each will use;
- settling a dispute with another child through negotiation, addressing their own rights as well as accommodating the other child's needs (for example, "I'll use the paste for these two pieces of paper and then give it to you");
- using words suggested by an adult to settle conflicts.

First Grade

1 **Uses simple strategies to make social decisions and solve problems.**

Learning how to make constructive social decisions and resolve differences of opinion is an important and challenging task for children and requires extensive modeling and guidance from adults. For six year olds, using words to resolve conflicts and knowing when to ask for help (rather than reacting impulsively) is an indication of a child's developing skills. Examples include:

- negotiating with another child, using words to express personal feelings;
- listening to another point of view and considering ways to compromise;
- discussing with two other children how to include a new member in their game;
- seeking teacher assistance when game participants cannot agree on the rules;
- dealing with feelings of anger by using the words suggested by an adult;
- seeking teacher advice about a problem with a friend and then using the strategy the teacher suggests.

Second Grade

1 **Uses simple strategies to make social decisions and solve problems.**

Learning how to make constructive social decisions and resolve differences in ideas and opinions is an important and challenging task and requires extensive modeling and guidance from adults. By second grade, most children can talk over problems, describe their feelings, and consider different options. Because fairness is so important to them, a great deal of time is often needed to discuss and debate disagreements. Knowing when to ask for help and being able to use it are signs of maturity in second graders. Some examples include:

- discussing with a peer the pros and cons of using different ways to signify water in a river model, then deciding on a method agreeable to both;
- accepting help from an adult other than the teacher (para-professional, special subject teacher) when dealing with feelings of anger;
- seeking teacher assistance when a project work group encounters seemingly irreconcilable differences;
- negotiating with another child about how to use a computer program.

Third Grade

1 **Uses strategies to make social decisions and solve social problems.**

Learning how to make constructive social decisions and resolve differences in ideas and opinions is an important and challenging task for children and requires extensive modeling and guidance from adults. Most third graders can talk over problems, describe their feelings, and consider options. They rely on various strategies for conflict resolution, including getting help from an adult or peer or using class meetings as a forum for problem-solving. Some examples of growth in this area include:

- using words that defend one's personal rights and beliefs when negotiating with another child;
- debating the outcome of a competitive game and then agreeing on a new way to play more fairly the next time;
- making independent decisions despite peer pressure to do something else (such as deciding to draw a mural even though close friends will be playing a board game);
- bringing up a problem that occurs outside the classroom (in the gym or at recess) for class discussion.

I Personal and Social Development

Language and Literacy

This domain organizes the language and literacy skills needed to understand and convey meaning into five components: Listening, Speaking, Reading, Writing, and Research. Students acquire proficiency in this domain through extensive experience with language, print, and literature in a variety of contexts. Over time students learn to construct meaning, make connections to their own lives, and gradually begin to critically analyze and interpret what they hear, observe, and read. They begin to communicate effectively orally and in writing for different audiences and purposes.

Preschool-3

1 Gains meaning by listening.

Three year olds learn about their world through watching and listening. They find it easier to listen with understanding in one-on-one situations than in groups. The ability to listen in a group emerges slowly and with practice. They can listen to familiar stories and videos for relatively longer periods of time than when they are asked to attend to unfamiliar materials. Three year olds show their understanding by:

- listening attentively to stories read aloud;
- listening briefly to other people's conversations and responding to the content;
- listening to short, familiar records and tapes, and showing understanding through body language (clapping or nodding) or facial expressions (smiling or laughing);
- conversing with a teacher and responding appropriately;
- listening to a visitor tell about what she does in the community and later using the words and content in dramatic play.

Preschool-4

1 Gains meaning by listening.

Four year olds gain knowledge about their world by watching and listening. They acquire the skill to listen not only when they are spoken to one-on-one by adults and peers, but also to listen when they are spoken to as part of a group. This "group listening skill" is important for learning and acquiring information in school settings. Listening with understanding is enhanced as stories are read to large and small groups and as children participate in singing and chanting activities. Children show their developing listening skills by:

- carrying on a conversation with another person that extends a thought or idea expressed to the group earlier;
- responding to stories read to the whole class, rather than responding only when read to as part of a small group;
- understanding a change in the morning activity schedule described by the teacher;
- watching and listening to a video and discussing the story later in the day;
- listening to audio-taped stories and showing understanding through body language, pointing to appropriate pictures, or retelling what they heard.

Kindergarten

1 Gains meaning by listening.

Young children are actively involved in learning about their world by watching and listening. At five years, children can listen for meaning in such different situations as one-on-one conversations with children or adults, small and large group activities, story times, and videos. They demonstrate their attentiveness through body language, eye contact, and active participation. They show their understanding by asking questions, making comments relevant to the topic, and reacting appropriately to what is heard. Children demonstrate their listening skills by:

- using information from a story about transportation to create a city in the block area;
- asking a question to clarify their understanding of a video about bears;
- showing understanding during a group discussion by leaning forward, frowning, or smiling;
- recognizing the intent behind the words of peers (for example, accepting an apology given for causing an accident);
- understanding the message or story expressed in a book, audiotape or CD-ROM.

First Grade

1 Gains meaning by listening.

By listening, observing, and analyzing information critically, children gain understanding of the world around them. First graders are increasingly able to listen to stories read aloud, gain information, and hear directions and rules. They can listen for pleasure, information, and social interaction one-on-one, as well as in small or large groups. They can often sit for extended periods of time listening to a "good" story or presentation, but may squirm and fidget if asked to attend to something that does not immediately capture their interest. Examples of how they gain meaning by listening include:

- listening to a story read aloud and relating it to a personal experience;
- listening to a book read aloud and asking or answering a relevant question;
- listening critically as a peer retells the part of the book they heard yesterday and adding some details that she left out;
- demonstrating attentiveness and comprehension as a listener through body language or facial expressions (for example, nodding in agreement, laughing at a joke).

Second Grade

1 Gains meaning by listening.

By listening, observing, and critically analyzing information, children gain understanding of the world around them. Most second graders can listen to the ideas of others to gain information and for pleasure and enjoyment. They can pay attention to and understand what they hear in small and large groups, asking specific questions to clarify or extend meaning. Examples of how they demonstrate these skills include:

- demonstrating attentiveness and comprehension as a listener by means of body language or facial expressions;
- listening to a guest speaker and then incorporating some details from the presentation into a story;
- asking a question for clarification after listening to a classmate's story;
- paraphrasing information presented orally by a teacher or peer;
- using new vocabulary words in conversation and writing after hearing them read aloud in a story;
- listening as a peer tells how to solve a math problem and then questioning the logic of the method described.

Third Grade

1 Gains meaning by listening.

Third graders can listen attentively and focus on the speaker in small and large group settings. They can summarize and paraphrase what they have heard, ask questions for elaboration or clarification, and follow multi-step directions independently. Examples of these skills include:

- asking for clarification of an idea during a group discussion;
- paraphrasing classmates' viewpoints expressed during a conflict;
- relaying directions about an assignment given earlier in the week to a friend who was absent;
- listening to an explanation given by a museum docent and then retelling details during a discussion back in the classroom;
- listening to someone explain the directions for a software program and then using the program successfully;
- listening to a short lecture and taking some notes.

II Language and Literacy

Language and Literacy

Preschool-3

2 **Follows two-step directions.**

Three year olds still need substantial individual support, instruction, and physical guidance to be able to follow directions. They show skills in this area by:

- following directions given to them specifically (such as, "Please pick up that toy and put it on the shelf.");
- remembering to clean up their place at lunch after eating;
- matching movements and actions to the music and directions in a song;
- following the teacher's simple directions to the class (for example, "Find a book and take it to your table.") without needing individual clarification;
- putting on their coats when reminded it is time to go home and remembering to take their backpacks.

Preschool-4

2 **Follows two- or three-step directions.**

Remembering and following directions is critical for preschool children's independent functioning in educational settings. Four year olds are beginning to follow simple two- and three-step directions with relative ease. They also respond to group directions rather than always needing individual instruction. Four year olds show they can follow directions by:

- responding to the instruction to the class, "Go get your coats and when you are dressed, sit down on the rug";
- repeating an instruction to a friend;
- following directions on a tape or CD to perform various movements;
- following directions given to the class to "Take this note about our class trip home, ask your family to read it, have a family member sign it, and bring it back to me";
- following directions given by the teacher to "Go wash your hands and then sit down at the table."

Kindergarten

2 **Follows directions that involve a series of actions.**

Five year olds can follow three-step directions immediately after they hear them, but sometimes forget instructions over time or become distracted before they can complete a longer series of actions. The ability to focus and remember is important for school success. Children demonstrate their growing ability to follow directions by:

- understanding teacher directions given to the class without needing to ask the teacher to repeat what to do;
- following a set of instructions without reminders (for example, going out to recess without forgetting any steps in the routine);
- leaving the classroom earlier than other children to deliver a message to the school secretary and then meeting the class at the door to the playground;
- remembering instructions given earlier (for example, going to the circle area after snack today, rather than to the quiet reading area as usual);
- relating a set of instructions to a classmate.

First Grade

2 Follows multi-step directions.

Six year olds can understand and follow three- to four-step oral directions. Because they often forget or become distracted before completing a set of instructions, gentle and frequent reminders enable them to follow through to completion. Examples of how children demonstrate their increasing skill in following directions include:

- listening to someone give a series of related instructions and following them without a reminder;
- delivering a note from the teacher to the office and then waiting for an answer from the secretary before returning to the classroom;
- helping a classmate who did not hear or understand the directions by carefully repeating them;
- listening to a friend explain the directions for a game and then playing it with few reminders about what to do next;
- hearing the choices for work time, making a decision about what to do, and then following through with the choice.

Second Grade

2 Follows multi-step directions.

Second graders can understand and follow three- to four-step oral directions with increasing independence. When asked, they can restate the directions accurately. Examples of how they demonstrate this skill are:

- listening to a series of related instructions for an activity and following them accurately;
- repeating the steps for an assignment to a classmate who was out of the room when they were given;
- listening to someone explain the directions for a software program and then using the program successfully;
- teaching a peer how to play a game shortly after having just heard how to play it;
- inventing a geoboard game and explaining the directions to others.

Third Grade

2 Critically analyzes what is heard or seen.

Most third graders are able to listen critically and interpret what they see and hear. They can compare different ideas and points of view and connect personal experiences with those they hear about and observe. They can begin to recognize strategies that affect how messages are perceived (for example, sound effects, background music, color and light in the media). Examples include:

- listening to a classmate reading a story in progress and offering specific suggestions for improving it;
- listening to an advertisement and identifying the persuasive message it contains;
- describing the author's use of metaphors in a story read aloud;
- relating relevant personal experiences to information shared by a friend;
- describing how music created a mood in a play presented by the fifth grade class;
- helping to mediate a conflict between peers by pointing out what is fact and opinion in each side's arguments.

Preschool-3

3 Shows beginning phonological awareness

Phonological awareness is the ability to hear and discriminate the sounds of language. Three year olds spontaneously play with the sounds of words and show some awareness of rhyming sounds. Examples of phonological awareness include:

- repeating familiar rhyming verses or songs;
- joining in with other children to recite rhymes and poems at circle time;
- using rhythm sticks to tap out the syllables in their names;
- experimenting with sounds to make nonsense words ("spaghetti, baghetti, laghetti");
- clapping to represent the syllables of short phrases (for example, "We like pizza.").

Preschool-4

3 Demonstrates phonological awareness.

Phonological awareness refers to the ability to hear and discriminate the sounds of language. Four year olds can attend to and distinguish the smaller units of sound within words with teacher support. They can begin to hear and discriminate syllables, the beginning sounds of words, and rhyming sounds, prerequisite skills for being able to decode words when reading. Children show developing phonological awareness by:

- listening to the word the teacher says and then finding a word to rhyme with it;
- hearing the sound of the first letter in their own names and using this ability to sound out or "read" classmates' names that begin with the same letter;
- experimenting with words, giving them new beginning sounds;
- clapping out the number of syllables in their names;
- saying the sound of a letter when they see it in a new word because they recognize it from a familiar word (for example, the "s" sound in "stop").

Kindergarten

3 Demonstrates beginning phonemic awareness.

For children to become fluent readers, they must be able to hear the smallest units of sound within words (phonemes) and to focus on these sounds separate from the meaning of the word. With frequent demonstrations by the teacher, children recognize and produce rhyming words, identify beginning and ending sounds, and begin to discriminate the smaller parts of words, first distinguishing syllables and, later, phonemes within syllables. Examples include:

- announcing that Marc's and Matt's names begin with the same sound as Mike's name;
- identifying two words that rhyme, given a series of three words;
- knowing that words are made up of sounds and being able to identify the smallest units of sound (phonemes) in a word (for example "cat" has three phonemes: /c/ /a/ /t/);
- naming the word left when you take away the /b/ from "bat";
- sorting pictures of objects into two groups based on their beginning sounds.

First Grade

3 Demonstrates phonemic awareness.

Phonemic awareness refers to the ability to hear, think about, and manipulate the sounds in words. First graders who become successful readers can hear the smallest units of sound within words (phonemes), recognize sound segments (letter clusters, syllables), and know that words are made up of sequences of sounds. Some ways they show their ability to blend or segment phonemes include:

• hearing three distinct sounds within a word (for example, /b/ /a/ /t/ makes the word "bat");

• telling if a word sounds like another word in some way (starts the same, ends the same, or rhymes);

• saying three other words that begin with the same sound as "milk";

• counting the number of syllables in a word;

• noticing the rhyming pattern in a story the teacher reads aloud;

• adding or deleting sounds in spoken words to make new words (for example, removing the "s" from "stop" to make the new word "top");

• inventing a new verse to a rhyming poem.

Second Grade

See the following indicator on page 47 in Language and Literacy:

C Reading

2 Decodes unfamiliar words.

Third Grade

See the following indicator on page 47 in Language and Literacy:

C Reading

2 Analyzes words and acquires new vocabulary from reading.

II Language and Literacy

II Language and Literacy

Preschool-3

1 Speaks clearly enough to be understood by most listeners.

Three year olds usually speak in short sentences. Articulation errors may be present, but speech is usually clear enough to be understood with little difficulty. When three year olds are given many opportunities to talk, the length and complexity of their sentences increase. Speaking clearly for three year olds includes:

- requesting information and being understood;

- describing a recent event and answering questions about it;

- signing or using a communication board to indicate their food choices at snack;

- initiating a conversation with an adult;

- telling a story using words, props, and gestures to convey meaning.

Preschool-4

1 Speaks clearly enough to be understood without contextual clues.

By four years of age, children usually speak with sufficient clarity so that it is easy to understand what they are saying without the help of additional information or gestures. Four year olds generally use correct syntax, but sometimes over generalize rules (for example, "We *goed* to the store."). Although they may still make some articulation errors, the length of their utterances and the grammatical complexity of their language is increasing. Evidence of this includes:

- speaking clearly enough so that a classroom visitor knows what they are saying;

- accurately delivering a message from home to the teacher;

- using common social conventions, such as "please" or "thank you," although often needing reminders;

- communicating in a way that other children understand what is being said without constantly having to ask, "What did you say?";

- telling the class about the trip to visit their grandmother;

- using sign language to indicate who they want to sit next to on the trip to the apple orchard.

Kindergarten

1 Speaks clearly and conveys ideas effectively.

At five, most children's speech is easily understood by listeners. During kindergarten, children begin to understand how to express their ideas coherently in group discussions as well as in one-to-one conversations. They speak loudly enough to be heard by their listeners. Their sentences become longer and more complex as their language becomes richer and more detailed. Children show emergent skills in this area by:

- retelling the morning events in more than short phrases;

- asking "how" and "why" questions in sentence form rather than by using only a word or two;

- initiating conversations with peers about what they did over the weekend;

- participating in conversations around the snack table or on the playground, speaking loudly enough to be heard by the group;

- relaying a message from the teacher to the school nurse;

- explaining why they think snowflakes melt more quickly than ice cubes.

First Grade

1 Speaks clearly and conveys ideas effectively.

When given numerous opportunities for exploratory conversations and discussions, most first graders can speak so others can understand them, adjusting volume and expression appropriately. They attempt to stay focused on a topic. With encouragement from a teacher, they can express ideas in complete sentences using simple and accurate syntax. Some ways they demonstrate speaking skills include:

- speaking clearly and audibly when telling the class about something that happened over the weekend;
- asking a question to get more information about the topic being discussed;
- using expression to emphasize a point of view;
- initiating a conversation with a classmate about a television show they both watched;
- reading their own writing to the class so that others can hear and understand it,
- making a relevant comment about a character in a story.

Second Grade

1 Speaks clearly and conveys ideas effectively.

Most second graders can stay focused on a topic in discussions and conversations and can respond with relevant questions and comments. When given opportunities for conversations and discussions throughout the day, they begin to include an increasing number of details and use more complex sentences when describing events and ideas. Examples of this include:

- making relevant contributions to class discussions;
- posing a question to get clarification about an assignment;
- asking a clarifying question after listening to a classmate's story;
- telling the class in detail about a recent family hiking trip;
- recounting a funny story to a group of friends;
- using complete sentences to express an opinion about the motive of a character in a story.

Third Grade

1 Speaks effectively using increasingly precise vocabulary.

When given opportunities for conversations and discussions throughout the day, most third graders can speak clearly, varying tone and volume appropriately to the situation. They can differentiate between formal and informal language. When speaking to a group, they can begin to organize their ideas before speaking. They are increasingly able to use descriptive vocabulary when they speak for different purposes (for example, to inform, persuade, entertain, and express opinions and feelings). Examples of third grade speaking skills include:

- using precise language to express ideas, opinions, and feelings related to group discussions;
- enhancing an oral presentation by using facial expressions, pauses and gestures, and changing vocal tones;
- using specific language to explain the solution to a math problem;
- trying out in conversation a new vocabulary word acquired from reading;
- engaging in debates and offering persuasive arguments;
- using language (puns, riddles, jokes) to express humor.

Preschool-3

2 Uses expanded vocabulary and language for a variety of purposes.

Children this age are fascinated with language and enjoy experimenting with sounds and expressions. Their vocabulary is developing rapidly. Although three year olds understand that they are expected to respond when someone speaks to them, they are only beginning to acquire other conversational rules (taking turns, staying on topic). They are gaining an understanding of the power of words and the excitement of communicating. Examples of their emerging skills include:

- using the word "tremendous" learned from a Dr. Seuss book when telling a classmate about the amount of sand being piled up in the sand table;
- making up "silly" words (for example, doggie, froggie, soggy, toggy, loggy);
- making up dialogue for a role-play in the dramatic play corner;
- relating an event from a trip to the fire station to something being read aloud from a book;
- telling someone about a recent trip to the hardware store or a park.

Preschool-4

2 Uses expanded vocabulary and language for a variety of purposes.

Four year olds are expanding their vocabulary daily through exposure to books, trips, and other classroom activities. At the same time, they are beginning to converse about objects and events that are not physically present, are somewhat abstract, or that they remember from the past. They are learning the social rules for conversation, but continue to have difficulty staying on topic in a group discussion. By this age, children are proficient enough with speech and language skills so that they can be creative and humorous in their explorations of how words work and sound. Examples include:

- waiting for their turn to speak before announcing the arrival of their new puppy;
- using words to communicate their feelings;
- telling a classroom visitor about the different trucks in the truck area, using the appropriate terminology;
- adding a relevant idea to another child's comment;
- telling jokes and giggling, even though they do not understand the significance of the word relationships in jokes and puns (for example, Knock-Knock jokes).

Kindergarten

2 Uses expanded vocabulary and language for a variety of purposes.

During kindergarten, children's expanding vocabularies provide them with a larger knowledge base that will assist them as they begin to read. They are acquiring words to name or describe many different things, and they are refining their social use of language by initiating conversations, taking turns in group discussions, and asking questions and making comments related to topics being discussed. Five year olds continue to use language for many purposes, such as playing with the sounds of language, reciting poems and rhymes, giving directions, explaining events, describing objects, and asking questions. Examples include:

- trying out a new word learned at morning circle later in the day while playing in the block area;
- telling a joke to a friend or making up new jokes, such as a "Knock-Knock" joke;
- waiting for their turn before talking about their favorite movie;
- initiating a conversation with a visitor to the classroom;
- asking questions relevant to an event reported by another child.

First Grade

2 Uses expanded vocabulary and language for a variety of purposes.

As first graders expand their vocabularies, they are increasingly comfortable expressing themselves in different situations and for different purposes. They offer explanations, ask questions, and share knowledge, ideas, and opinions. First graders are beginning to recognize the difference between questions and comments. Socially, they greet others, make their needs known, talk with peers and adults, and invite others to join a group. Creatively, they try to make rhymes, tell jokes and riddles, sing, and use expression when dramatizing a story. Examples include:

- trying out a new vocabulary word while telling or writing a story;
- asking a question for clarification after listening to a peer read a story to the class;
- making up a new verse to a familiar song;
- describing with some detail what was observed in a science experiment;
- learning new words by playing rhyming games;
- using appropriate words to express feelings of pleasure, sadness, anger, or frustration to peers and adults.

Second Grade

2 Uses expanded vocabulary and language for a variety of purposes.

Second graders can differentiate between formal and informal language. Their increasing vocabularies enable them to be more precise when speaking in order to inform, persuade, give directions, entertain, and express personal opinions and feelings. Examples of their skills include:

- using colorful and imaginative language as a way to enhance descriptions;
- using specific names or labels for objects rather than calling them "things" or "stuff";
- telling jokes and riddles or making plays on words;
- using expressive language to narrate skits or dramatize scenes;
- giving specific directions to a classmate about how to use a new computer program;
- using vocabulary words appropriate to the topic when presenting an oral report to the class.

Third Grade

See the following indicator on page 39 in Language and Literacy:

B Speaking

1 Speaks effectively using increasingly precise vocabulary.

Preschool-3

1 Shows appreciation for books.

Three year olds can become very excited about books, especially if they are exposed to literature before coming to school. Children's interest in a specific story or topic, the appropriateness of the text and illustrations, and the size of the group are key factors in their ability to sit still and stay focused during story reading. Children learn during preschool that books are handled in particular ways. Three year olds show their developing appreciation of books by:

- paying attention to a story read in a small group and responding to questions about the story;

- holding a book right side up and turning pages one at a time starting at the front of the book;

- choosing to join a small group that is listening to a story;

- acting out various parts in *Ask Mr. Bear* or *Are You My Mother?* as the teacher reads the story;

- recognizing a favorite book by its cover and asking that it be read to them.

Preschool-4

1 Shows appreciation for books and reading.

Depending on how often they have been read to at home and in other situations, children come to preschool with varying abilities to enjoy and understand the written word. By four, children can begin to learn about authors and illustrators, and enjoy making their own books. Children are encouraged to want to read when they are read to, taught how to handle books, and asked to respond to stories. Children show interest in books and in reading by:

- recognizing specific books by their covers;

- looking at books in an orderly fashion, turning one page at a time, going from front to back;

- pretending to read by pointing to words with one finger as they recite the text;

- listening or attending to a story without becoming distracted;

- asking questions about the details of a story just heard;

- improvising dialogue for the re-enactment of a story in the dramatic play area;

- asking to have a favorite book read during choice time;

- creating voices for characters in books.

Kindergarten

1 Shows interest in and knowledge about books and reading.

Children enter school with varying levels of experience with and interest in books and reading. Through repeated exposure to literature, kindergarten children can be expected to understand that authors write books, illustrators draw pictures, and books convey information or stories. Five year olds can listen attentively to stories and develop preferences for books by certain authors or topics of special interest. Examples of their interest and knowledge include:

- during free play, choosing to listen to an audiotape of the story the teacher read during group time;

- using books to find out about road-building machinery or to locate the name of a particular dinosaur;

- pretending to read a book using pictures or memory as cues;

- noticing that the book they are looking at has the same kind of drawings as a Richard Scarry book they have at home;

- listening attentively to a story and saying why they liked that story.

First Grade

1 Shows interest in books and reading.

Appreciating books and reading helps children become life-long readers. A wide variety of reading-related activities in the classroom provides first graders meaningful opportunities to cultivate an interest and enthusiasm for reading and to practice their emerging skills. At this age, children's interest in books and print sometimes exceeds their reading abilities. Examples of growing interest include:

- bringing in a book from home and asking the teacher to read it aloud to the class;
- stopping to look at the print and pictures on the bulletin board in the hallway outside the classroom;
- selecting a non-fiction book related to a personal interest to check out from the school's library;
- borrowing a favorite book from the classroom library to take home to re-read with a parent;
- finding a book about alligators in order to make an accurate drawing for a science project;
- looking for other books in the class library written by the author of the book they just finished reading.

Second Grade

1 Shows interest in books and reading.

Appreciating books and reading leads to becoming a life-long reader. Second graders choose to spend extended periods of time engaged in reading-related activities. Their interest in books and reading may sometimes exceed their reading abilities. Some examples of increasing interest are:

- selecting books or magazines to look at and read for pleasure;
- playing games that involve reading words and sentences;
- choosing to listen to a book on tape at the listening center;
- looking for books related to a personal interest (for example, baseball, horses, or dinosaurs);
- listening with interest and concentration to stories read to them;
- using new vocabulary gained from reading a story;
- finishing a book and then seeking another by the same author.

Third Grade

1 Shows interest in books and reading.

Appreciating books and reading leads to becoming a life-long reader. By third grade, interested and excited readers choose to read for extended periods of time, talk about books, and use books as resources. Some third graders' skill levels are not equal to their interest in books and reading. Examples of how third graders show interest in literature and reading include:

- reading several books of the same genre (mysteries, biographies, science fiction);
- finding and reading information on the Internet about a topic of interest;
- using free time in the classroom for reading;
- incorporating ideas from a story they have read into their own writing;
- sharing, reviewing, and recommending books to others;
- borrowing and reading books from the school library;
- selecting books based on personal interests and preferences.

Preschool-3

2 Shows interest in letters and words.

By the age of three, children are beginning to become aware of how letters and words look and sound. They may show interest in letters, especially the letters in their names. They notice labels and signs in their environment and ask caregivers and teachers what the signs say. Examples of their interest and participation in reading-related activities include:

- saying, "There's my name!" when they see a stop sign because their name begins with the letter "S";
- pointing to classroom labels and "reading" the word printed there (for example, "fish," "clock," "puzzles")—although not recognizing the same word if it appears somewhere else;
- asking, "What does that say?" when they see a sign, label or other print;
- picking out and labeling specific letters from their names as they look at book titles or classroom labels;
- identifying their names on their toothbrushes or cubbies;
- pointing to a logo and reading the name of the supermarket or the brand of crackers;
- singing the alphabet song.

Preschool-4

2 Shows beginning understanding of concepts about print.

Four year olds are beginning to learn how print works. They understand that speech can be written down and then read, and that the print on a page conveys the story. They have some awareness that reading is done from top to bottom and left to right, and are beginning to acquire the concept of "a word." Four year olds understand that print takes different forms (for example, grocery lists, signs, stories) and that it can be read for enjoyment as well as for informational purposes. Children demonstrate a growing understanding of print by:

- protesting when a different version of a familiar story is read because they know that the words in a storybook do not change;
- asking the teacher for help in making a sign for the dramatic play area that says "Doctor's Office" or "Clinic";
- pointing to words using a left to right progression when "reading" picture books;
- writing a series of scribbles separated by spaces under a drawing of a truck;
- checking the classroom job chart to find out whose job it is to feed the gerbil.

Kindergarten

2 Shows some understanding of concepts about print.

Five year olds are beginning to understand how print is organized and read. They realize that print conveys meaning, spoken language can be written down and read, and certain words are always written the same way. They begin to notice spaces between words, distinguish letters from drawings and numerals, recognize different types of text (storybooks, poems, newspapers, grocery lists, signs, letters, labels), label the parts of a book (front cover, title page, back cover), and track print from left to right and top to bottom, pointing to the words as they are read. Examples include:

- finding the front of the book, turning to the first page of text before they begin reading, pointing to where the teacher should begin reading, and then turning the pages one by one;
- sweeping a finger from left to right across print on a page as they "read" a favorite story from memory;
- asking whether they are the "author" of the story they dictated to the teacher;
- listening to an audiotape and following along in the book, turning the pages at the correct time.

First Grade

2 Shows understanding of concepts about print.

To become successful readers, first graders need basic knowledge about print and books, including how print is organized (from left to right and top to bottom) and the parts of books (front and back cover, title page, author, and illustrator). When looking at print, they can differentiate between letters, words, and sentences and recognize some basic punctuation marks. They know that writing is used for different purposes. Some examples are:

• noting the title and author of the story on the front cover of the book;

• pointing to each word when reading;

• recognizing an unusual pattern in a book where the text goes straight across two pages, rather than straight down on one page;

• including a separate title page in their own writing;

• reading aloud, stopping at an exclamation mark, and then re-reading the sentence with expression;

• looking over a story just written and recognizing that a space is missing between two words and a period is needed at the end of the sentence.

Second Grade

See the following indicator on page 49 in Language and Literacy:

C Reading

3 Uses strategies to construct meaning from print.

Third Grade

See the following indicator on page 49 in Language and Literacy:

C Reading

3 Uses strategies to construct meaning from print.

II Language and Literacy

45

Preschool-3

See the following indicator on page 44 in Language and Literacy:

C Reading

2 Shows interest in letters and words.

Preschool-4

3 Begins to develop knowledge about letters.

As four year olds are exposed to books and other forms of writing, their interest in letters increases. Although they initially feel that they "own" letters ("that's my 'S'") or confuse letters with numerals and other symbols, they soon realize that letters are the building blocks of words. With continued adult guidance, they can learn the names of letters, identify some letters in varied contexts, and match a few sounds with letters. They show increasing knowledge about letters by:

- differentiating and correctly identifying some letters by their shapes;
- recognizing letters in a specific context only (for example, labeling the "K" in K-Mart, but not the "K" in Kathy);
- guessing a word by recognizing its initial letter ("reads" all words beginning with "s" as "stop");
- announcing, "My name and Tonya's name start with the letter 'T'";
- identifying upper case letters as they sing the alphabet song;
- naming the letters in their first names as they attempt to write their names.

Kindergarten

3 Knows letters, sounds, and how they form words.

By the end of kindergarten, children acquire knowledge about the systematic relationship between letters and sounds. They understand that a group of letters represents a sequence of sounds that combine to form a word (the alphabetic principle). Kindergartners can identify and name uppercase and lowercase letters, understand that letters stand for sounds, and associate the correct sound with many letters. They begin to sound out simple words and can develop a limited sight vocabulary. Five year olds demonstrate these skills by:

- picking out their names on classroom lists and beginning to recognize their friends' names;
- pointing out the letter "k" in the sign for kitchen;
- recognizing familiar words on the cover of a favorite book;
- developing a personal list of words they can recognize on sight;
- occasionally sounding out simple words as they write in journals or make captions for pictures;
- beginning to "read" a favorite book using pictures as clues and gradually recognizing words that are repeated in the text.

First Grade

3 Decodes unfamiliar words.

By the end of the year, most first graders know the sounds made by each letter of the alphabet and use letter-sound correspondence to sound out unknown words when reading (phonics). With single syllable words, most children this age can distinguish initial, medial, and final sounds; long and short vowel sounds; and blends and digraphs. With encouragement, they can figure out unfamiliar words by examining their structures (for example, recognizing familiar clusters of letters, prefixes and suffixes, or patterns in words). Examples include:

- successfully reading the word "snack" on the morning message by saying the beginning blend, the short /a/, and the ending sound;
- reading the word "stopping" correctly by recognizing the familiar word "stop" and the suffix "ing";
- suggesting the teacher use "hug" in the class poem because it rhymes with "bug" and then spelling it correctly for the chart;
- reading or writing a word list in which the words share a spelling sound pattern (for example, man, pan, ran, can).

Second Grade

2 Decodes unfamiliar words.

Second graders use phonics skills (their knowledge of the sounds made by letters and groups of letters) to help them read unfamiliar words. Most children this age can decode multi-syllabic words accurately using beginning sounds, letter clusters, and blends. They use word patterns and the structure of words (including prefixes, suffixes, and endings) to help them read unfamiliar words and expand their vocabularies. Examples of how they apply decoding skills include:

- figuring out the meaning of a compound word by analyzing its parts;
- using knowledge of homonyms to figure out words and expand vocabulary;
- sorting words by the words' ending patterns ("ies," "ed," "ing");
- using knowledge of vowel patterns (for example, long "e," "ee," "ea") to figure out unknown words;
- figuring out the meaning of the word "unicycle" by recognizing the root word "cycle" and then the prefix "uni";
- using the word pattern "tion" to help them read the unfamiliar word "station."

Third Grade

2 Analyzes words and acquires new vocabulary from reading.

Third graders progress from decoding to analyzing words by focusing on the parts of words. Most third graders can analyze the structure of words using root words, prefixes, suffixes, and word families. They begin to grasp the patterns and complexities of the English language system, including parts of speech and categories of words (synonyms, homophones, homographs, antonyms, compound words, and multiple meaning words). They also can be encouraged to use a dictionary to learn the meaning of new words. As their reading vocabularies expand, they begin to use new words. Examples include:

- using decoding and syllabication to pronounce an unfamiliar word correctly;
- using prefixes (for example, /un/, /re/, /pre/, /bi/) and suffixes (for example, /er/, /est/, /ful/) to figure out word meanings;
- decoding words using more complex word families (for example, /ight/, /ought/);
- struggling to decode an unfamiliar word encountered in a reference book and then using the dictionary to find out the meaning.

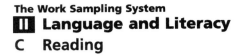

II Language and Literacy

C Reading

Preschool-3	Preschool-4	Kindergarten

Preschool-3

Not expected at this level.

Preschool-4

Not expected at this level.

Kindergarten

See the following indicator on page 44 in Language and Literacy:

C Reading

2 Shows some understanding of concepts about print.

See the following indicator on page 46 in Language and Literacy:

C Reading

3 Knows letters, sounds, and how they form words.

See the following indicator on page 50 in Language and Literacy:

C Reading

4 Comprehends and responds to fiction and non-fiction text.

First Grade

4 Uses strategies to construct meaning from print.

Readers rely on many different strategies to help them make sense of text. With guidance from teachers, first graders learn to look for cues related to meaning, language structure, and visual information to help them understand what they read. They are beginning to monitor themselves as they read to be sure that what they have read makes sense, and they attempt to self-correct when it does not. Some ways first graders use reading strategies include:

- using a picture to figure out an unfamiliar word (for example, looking at both the picture of a mosquito and at the word, making the /m/ sound, and then saying the word "mosquito");
- skipping a word or making a guess and then figuring it out based on the meaning of the story;
- reading a sentence, then stopping and saying, "This doesn't sound right," and re-reading it correctly;
- asking a question to try to make sense of the text when they don't understand what they've read;
- saying, "I knew it didn't make sense, so I read it again." in response to the teacher's question, "How did you figure it out?".

Second Grade

3 Uses strategies to construct meaning from print.

When reading grade level text, second graders use strategies with increasing skill to understand the literal meaning of the text. They look for cues to help them figure out the meaning of the text (for example, using context or structure, predicting, visualizing, reading on, attending to punctuation), monitor their reading to be sure that what they have read makes sense, and self-correct when it does not make sense. Examples include:

- re-reading a sentence when the meaning is not clear the first time;
- using prior knowledge to predict what the book will be about before reading;
- self-correcting after looking at a picture and realizing that although the misread word made sense in the sentence, it was not accurate;
- reading sight words easily and quickly;
- skipping a difficult sentence while reading and then going back later to figure out what was missed.

Third Grade

3 Uses strategies to construct meaning from print.

When reading grade-level text, third graders search for cues (meaning, structure, visual). They can self-monitor and self-correct at different times in the reading process. Examples of how they use these strategies include:

- making predictions about the text using title, chapter headings, and illustrations;
- skipping words that are unfamiliar and unimportant to the meaning of a story;
- using prior knowledge about a subject to figure out difficult words;
- identifying a phrase that gets in the way of understanding and grappling with it until it is understood;
- coming to an unfamiliar word, reading on, and then going back to figure out the meaning based on the rest of the paragraph;
- using the chapter headings of informational text to locate and make sense of the information.

II Language and Literacy

Preschool-3	Preschool-4	Kindergarten
3 Comprehends and responds to stories read aloud.	**4 Comprehends and responds to stories read aloud.**	**4 Comprehends and responds to fiction and non-fiction text.**

Three year olds are actively engaged in understanding stories. They begin to follow what characters say and do in a story. Frequently, children memorize some of the words of the story or can finish sentences in books that have repetitive patterns of phrases. Examples of their growing comprehension of stories includes:

- asking relevant questions as the story is read;

- labeling pictures in familiar books;

- recognizing when the reader omits part of a favorite story;

- pointing to pictures of characters in a story and recalling what the characters did or said;

- looking at books during free choice time, often talking out loud about them and telling a story that may or may not reflect the actual text;

- using pictures in a book to recall details about a story;

- retelling a story using flannel board cutouts or hand puppets.

As four year olds become involved with familiar stories, their comprehension grows. They begin retelling stories in a variety of ways (looking at the pictures and making up the text, acting out part of the story in dramatic play, or telling the story using a flannel board) and asking why things happened as they did. With teacher guidance, they can begin to guess or make predictions about what will happen next and to connect the story to their own experiences. Four year olds show their comprehension of stories by:

- acting out a familiar story with their classmates;

- asking questions and making comments about a story;

- retelling the main events of a story just read or told by the teacher;

- telling about when the family car was towed after hearing a story about a tow truck;

- guessing what will happen next by looking at the picture on the following page;

- commenting on the actions described in a story (guessing why the monkeys threw down the caps from the tree in *Caps for Sale*).

Kindergartners expand their vocabulary and general background knowledge as they listen to fiction and non-fiction texts read aloud. They demonstrate their understanding of what they hear by answering questions about the text, predicting what will happen next using pictures and content for guides, and retelling information from a story in sequence, adding more details and story elements over time. After children comprehend a text, they begin to relate their own experiences to what they have read. Examples include:

- looking at pictures in a book and predicting what will happen next;

- answering questions and adding their own comments about a story as it is being read;

- predicting what will happen to characters in a story based on the characters' actions thus far;

- guessing book or story content from the book's title and cover;

- retelling a story in sequential order (beginning, middle, and end).

First Grade

5 Comprehends and interprets fiction and non-fiction text.

Comprehension involves gaining an initial understanding, developing an interpretation, personally reflecting and responding, and extending or critically evaluating text. As first graders listen to or read stories or informational text, they can be encouraged to apply each of these processes. When prompted, they can retell the main events or ideas in sequence. They can identify the setting, main characters, main events, and problems in a story. They are learning to preview text, predict and confirm the facts, and integrate background information or prior knowledge. Examples include:

- predicting and justifying what will happen next in a story;
- using their own words to describe information learned from an expository text and connecting the information to prior knowledge or experience;
- reading and carrying out simple written instructions (for example, reading a recipe or directions for a game);
- describing why they liked a story;
- re-enacting part of a story as a puppet show or skit.

Second Grade

4 Comprehends and interprets fiction and non-fiction text.

Comprehension involves gaining an initial understanding, developing an interpretation, personally reflecting and responding, and extending or critically evaluating text. Second graders show understanding and interpretation as they identify the main idea, characters, setting, events, and problems in stories, and recall facts and details from informational text. With prompting, they can begin to answer "how" "why" and "what if" questions, consider cause and effect relationships, and connect and compare information or stories across texts. Examples of their increasing comprehension skills include:

- retelling the events of a story in sequence;
- recalling the main idea and a few details from an informational book;
- posing a question about why a particular story event occurred as it did and then offering a possible explanation;
- dramatizing a scene from a folktale and using some simple props to create the setting;
- pointing out the part of the book that is based on fact and comparing it with the part that is fiction.

Third Grade

4 Comprehends and interprets fiction and non-fiction text.

Comprehension involves gaining an initial understanding, developing an interpretation, personally reflecting and responding, and extending or critically evaluating text. Third graders can identify the main idea and supporting information. When reading fiction, they can recall the characters, setting, plot, problem, and solution, and explain feelings and opinions. With non-fiction, they can consider "why," "how" and "what if" questions. With encouragement, they can begin to relate ideas from one text to another, reflect on cause and effect relationships, distinguish between fact and opinion, and begin to recognize a variety of genres (for example, fables, folktales, fiction, non-fiction, or poetry). Examples include:

- identifying the main ideas after reading expository text;
- discussing a character's actions, motives, and emotions and relating them to personal feelings and experiences;
- depicting and describing scenes from a story by combining a variety of artistic media (drama, painting, poetry, songs) with oral or written language.

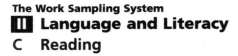

II Language and Literacy

C Reading

Preschool-3	Preschool-4	Kindergarten

Preschool-3

Not expected at this level.

Preschool-4

Not expected at this level.

Kindergarten

See the following indicator on page 42 in Language and Literacy:

C Reading

1 Shows interest in and knowledge about books and reading.

First Grade

See the following indicator on page 43 in Language and Literacy:

C Reading

1 Shows interest in books and reading.

See the following indicator on page 51 in Language and Literacy:

C Reading

5 Comprehends and interprets fiction and non-fiction text.

Second Grade

5 **Reads for varied purposes.**

As second graders begin to comprehend more difficult and varied text, they read for pleasure, to gain information, and to perform tasks or assignments. With encouragement, they can state their reasons for reading (for example, to learn the directions to a game or to read more books by the same author). Examples include:

- reading a book about whales to get answers to specific questions;
- reading books for pleasure at home and at school for extended periods of time;
- using the table of contents and chapter headings to locate information in books for a research project on squirrels;
- reading and comparing two different recipes for brownies and then deciding which one to make;
- using the computer to locate resources;
- reading sections about raccoons from three different books in order to prepare a report to present to the class;
- reviewing pictures in books about castles to help determine how to construct a model.

Third Grade

5 **Reads for varied purposes.**

Third graders can apply their knowledge and strategies while reading for pleasure and to gain information. They are familiar with a wide variety of literary genres and understand how to use informational text (for example, table of contents, chapter headings, indices). Examples of how third graders demonstrate the ability to read for a variety of purposes include:

- recognizing that the purpose of reading a computer magazine is both for pleasure and information, such as learning more about Internet access;
- distinguishing features of different genres (for example, the elements of fiction, the structure of fairy tales or mysteries);
- using reference books (dictionaries, encyclopedias) or electronic materials (for example, Internet, CD-ROMs) to gather information for a research project;
- reading non-fiction books to learn more about a topic of personal interest;
- enjoying a particular genre of literature (for example, historical fiction, folktales, biographies).

II Language and Literacy

II Language and Literacy

C Reading

Preschool-3

Not expected at this level.

Preschool-4

Not expected at this level.

Kindergarten

Not expected at this level.

First Grade

See the following indicator on page 42 in Language and Literacy:

C Reading

1 Shows interest in books and reading.

See the following indicator on page 51 in Language and Literacy:

C Reading

5 Comprehends and interprets fiction and non-fiction text.

Second Grade

6 Reads fluently and independently.

Second graders who are fluent readers no longer read word by word, but read easily and smoothly. Many children this age can read aloud using phrasing and expression. Occasionally, self-consciousness or shyness may get in the way of fluency when children read aloud. Examples of how second graders demonstrate fluency include:

- reading a familiar poem aloud with expression and attention to rhythm, flow, and meter;
- reading and comprehending grade-level-appropriate chapter books with ease;
- reading aloud and stumbling over a few words, but retelling the story with complete accuracy;
- reading picture books to kindergarten children with expression;
- reading aloud during literature circle and attempting to change their own voice to reflect different characters in the story;
- reading aloud to the class a letter from a pen pal.

Third Grade

6 Reads fluently and independently.

Third graders can read grade-level text independently, fluently, and for extended periods of time. They use phrasing and expression appropriately. Examples include:

- reading aloud to the class with expression;
- choosing to be the narrator for a skit and reading the script fluently and with expression;
- reading a difficult chapter book independently and then discussing details about the book with peers;
- reporting on current events after reading a newspaper article;
- reading a classroom announcement on the public address system smoothly and clearly;
- reading the directions for a new game to a small group before beginning to play the game.

Preschool-3

1 Represents ideas and stories through pictures, dictation, and play.

One of the first tasks in writing is to understand that letters are symbols that can be used to represent words, thoughts, and ideas. Three year olds are actively engaged in learning that symbols and pictures represent real things. For example, many know that the golden arches are a symbol for McDonalds. They understand that dolls can represent real people ("This is the mommy doll and this is the baby doll.") or that a play phone represents a real phone. They show their developing understanding of representation and symbols by:

- describing their drawings when the teacher says, "Tell me about your picture";
- listening on the toy phone and telling the teacher, "I'm talking with Mommy at work";
- covering a paper with large swirls of paint, telling the teacher, "This is my house," and asking the teacher to write "My House" on the painting;
- asking the teacher to write a note for their family telling about the visitor who brought a snake to class;
- making up a funny animal story using flannel cut outs to tell the story.

Preschool-4

1 Represents ideas and stories through pictures, dictation, and play.

Four year olds continue to investigate how symbols can stand for or represent other things. Before they can learn to write, children must first realize that letters and words are symbols which represent spoken words and stories. They know that labels on toy shelves tell where to put the toys, that the print in books tells the teacher what to read, and that their own drawings can represent their feelings, ideas, and experiences. They continue to gain experience with representation by:

- retelling the story *Caps for Sale* using cutouts of colored hat shapes;
- pretending to be a doctor in the dramatic play area and "writing" on a patient's chart;
- dictating a story about a picture and asking the teacher to write it down;
- building a block structure to represent the fire station in a story and asking the teacher for help writing "Fire Station";
- drawing a monster shape to go along with *There's a Monster in my Closet.*

Kindergarten

1 Represents stories through pictures, dictation, and play.

Many five year olds understand that words represent things, ideas, and events, and that letters make up words. They enjoy telling and "writing" stories. Long before they use conventional forms of writing, they willingly describe their drawings, use drawings to tell stories with a beginning, middle, and end, and represent stories as they play. They can focus on an idea for a story and make a simple plan for expressing it. Examples include:

- dramatizing a story about a mother and her children in the dramatic play area;
- dictating a story to the teacher about the class trip to the farm;
- sharing their drawing of a monster with a friend;
- building a city with small blocks and using pretend people to act out stories in the city;
- drawing the caterpillar from *The Very Hungry Caterpillar* and adding more details after talking about it with their teacher.

First Grade

See the following indicator on page 59 in Language and Literacy:

D Writing

1 Uses writing strategies to convey ideas.

Second Grade

See the following indicator on page 59 in Language and Literacy:

D Writing

1 Uses writing strategies to convey ideas.

Third Grade

See the following indicator on page 59 in Language and Literacy:

D Writing

1 Uses writing strategies to convey ideas.

Preschool-3

2 Uses scribbles and unconventional shapes to write.

Three year olds are beginning to understand that print can tell stories and express ideas. Although their initial attempts at writing are not conventional, they often make scribbles that begin at the top of the paper and move from left to right, showing their beginning understanding of how print works. Their first attempts at writing are shown by:

- scribbling on paper and describing the thoughts they have "written" down;
- drawing a round form and, after putting some red in the circle, announcing, "Here's an apple";
- making a sign consisting of several scribbles, and putting it in the block area to warn others to "Keep Out";
- scribbling letter-like marks on their pictures and reporting that they wrote their names;
- making several short wavy lines on the notepad in the dramatic play area to serve as a shopping list.

Preschool-4

2 Uses letter-like shapes, symbols, and letters to convey meaning.

As children observe the teacher making lists and putting names on art work, they often want to write for themselves. Position of letters on the paper, actual formation of the letters, and correct order are not yet part of most four year olds' repertoires. Many children become interested in writing their names and perhaps a few other significant words, while others will continue to ask for words to be written for them. Children's efforts to write at this age include:

- making rows of squiggles and shapes on a paper and calling it writing;
- labeling a drawing with several randomly placed letter-like shapes;
- writing their own names from memory on their art work;
- spontaneously writing uppercase letters they know;
- copying letters from signs and labels posted around the room, enjoying the power of doing "real writing";
- making shopping lists consisting of pictures, scribbles, and letter-like shapes in the dramatic play area before going to the grocery store;
- beginning to write several letters correctly.

Kindergarten

2 Uses letter-like shapes, symbols, letters, and words to convey meaning.

As children begin to understand that writing communicates a message, they become motivated to produce words, even if they do not possess conventional writing and spelling skills. They begin by using drawings to convey ideas, adding letters or words randomly. With experience, they begin to form words by using letters from their names, copying words, approaching others for help, sounding out words using letter-sound associations, and using invented or temporary spelling. By the end of kindergarten, many children can write most upper- and lowercase letters and know the conventional spelling for some words. Examples include:

- making marks that resemble letters, starting at the top left of the paper and moving from left to right and top to bottom;
- writing their names on their artwork;
- drawing a picture of a computer in their journal and using invented spelling to write "I LK CMPTRS";
- using invented spelling to form words with initial and final consonants.

First Grade

1 Uses writing strategies to convey ideas.

First graders benefit from having many opportunities to write throughout the day. They begin to demonstrate understanding of the writing process as they generate ideas, make simple plans, and develop main ideas that are supported with some detail and description. They are beginning to organize their writing in a sequence, including a basic beginning, middle, and end. Examples of first graders using writing strategies include:

- drawing on personal experiences to generate ideas for stories;
- hearing a story read aloud and using it as the basis for writing a story;
- brainstorming with a friend concerning what to write about;
- writing about going to the basketball game, staying focused on the topic, and including some details;
- drawing a picture of a favorite pet and then writing some sentences to go with the drawing;
- making a web before writing;
- folding a paper into thirds and drawing a picture in each third to help themselves clarify their ideas for the beginning, middle, and end of the story.

Second Grade

1 Uses writing strategies to convey ideas.

Second graders can apply simple strategies before writing (for example, generating ideas, making a plan) and develop a main idea with a few supporting details. They can develop an idea using several related sentences and, with prompting, organize related ideas into a few simple paragraphs. They are learning to sequence ideas in logical order, including a beginning, middle, and end. Examples of second graders applying these skills include:

- discussing ideas with a peer to help develop a plan for writing;
- making a web before writing;
- conferring with a friend and discussing which details to include in their writing;
- writing a few paragraphs describing a pet gerbil and including some humorous, descriptive language;
- writing a fiction story with a clear beginning, middle, and end;
- writing a letter describing a class project to a friend who just moved away.

Third Grade

1 Uses writing strategies to convey ideas.

With some guidance, third graders can use all aspects of the writing process to produce compositions and reports. They can focus on a central idea, include supportive details, be organized, and include transitions. Their prewriting strategies include using graphic organizers (for example, webs, story maps), making lists, grouping related ideas, and rehearsing ideas with peers. Although they understand the purpose of a first draft and that revision is necessary to create a satisfactory final product, they often need encouragement to go through all the steps of the writing process. Examples include:

- making a web before writing to organize ideas for a story;
- sequencing a story according to chronological events;
- writing several paragraphs related to a central focus and using transition words to link the paragraphs;
- adding relevant examples to illustrate the main points of an expository composition;
- writing a well-organized composition describing the similarities and differences between the main characters in a story.

Preschool-3

Not expected at this level.

Preschool-4

3 **Understands purposes for writing.**

Although four year olds do not write conventionally, their understanding of the power of writing is growing. Through repeated exposure to different types of writing and environmental print, they learn that writing can fulfill many different functions (for example, telling stories, conveying messages in a letter, describing the directions for a game) and that writing can be read for enjoyment as well as for information. Examples include:

- pretending to use a telephone book in the dramatic play area to find the phone number of a friend, then writing some numerals on a note pad;

- using letter stamps to represent words and then "reading" the message or story to another person;

- asking the teacher for help creating signs for the dramatic play area, such as "Hospital" or "Stay out";

- making grocery lists by writing lines across a note pad and taking the lists to the shopping center in the dramatic play area;

- drawing lines and squiggles across a page and asking the teacher to "Mail this letter to my friend Aisha."

Kindergarten

3 **Understands purposes for writing.**

Children begin to understand the power of written words when they see that messages, such as "Please Leave Standing" on a sign in front of a block structure, have an impact. Over time, they recognize that there are different types of writing (stories, signs, letters, lists) with different purposes. Children's understanding of writing as a symbolic form of communication that conveys messages motivates them to write on their own. Children exhibit this understanding by:

- realizing that a caption created for a picture or painting can tell a story about the image;

- making a sign, such as "Hospital" or "Shoe Store," for the dramatic play area;

- copying words to convey messages (for example, "Stop" or "Go");

- recognizing that putting their names on a product signifies that it was done by them;

- making lists of "things I like to do" or favorite songs;

- copying a note to take home;

- asking about the various signs used in the classroom (the "Exit" sign or the word "fish" on the fish tank).

First Grade

2 Writes for different purposes.

By the end of first grade, many children can write to describe events, provide information, tell stories, and respond to literature. When provided with numerous opportunities to write for different purposes, many first graders have a beginning understanding that they are writing for an audience and that the purpose of their writing affects organization and content. Examples are:

- drawing a picture and writing several sentences describing the class trip to the pumpkin farm;

- making a list of the children who will work on the mural;

- using software on the computer to draw and make captions for a family portrait;

- making a sign for the class museum that says "Our Collections";

- writing a "thank you" letter to the firefighter who visited the classroom;

- using funny words in their stories and explaining that they want to make the audience laugh.

Second Grade

2 Writes for different purposes in different formats.

Second graders are learning how to write to inform, explain, describe, tell stories, and respond to literature. They are developing an understanding that purpose and audience affect content and organization. Many second graders can write stories that include several literary elements (character, setting, problem, sequence of events, and resolution) and with assistance, can organize an informative report. Examples of second graders writing in different formats for different purposes include:

- using words and phrases to record information from a survey and then altering the format when writing a summary of the findings;

- writing a paragraph in a math journal describing how a math problem was solved;

- including most of the story elements in a story written over the course of several writing periods;

- writing a simple research report about birds of prey that follows a framework generated by the class concerning what to include and how to organize the information;

- rewriting a familiar story by changing the characters and setting.

Third Grade

2 Writes for different purposes in different formats.

Third graders write to question, inform, explain, describe, persuade, organize information, and entertain. They can write in different formats (for example, letters, advertisements, stories, reports, biographies, captions). As their reading experiences expand, they use voice, descriptive language, and tone to make their writing more effective. Examples include:

- composing a formal letter to a government official about an issue discussed in class and producing a final draft on the word processor;

- using descriptive words and figurative language effectively to elaborate details about the setting;

- creating a set of detailed written instructions about how to use a game invented with a peer;

- writing a research report that follows a particular framework or outline;

- including a metaphor in an original poem;

- writing a fictional story in the first person that incorporates many story elements (characters, setting, problem, sequence of events, resolution).

II Language and Literacy

▌▌ Language and Literacy
D Writing

Preschool-3	Preschool-4	Kindergarten

Preschool-3

Not expected at this level.

Preschool-4

Not expected at this level.

Kindergarten

See the following indicator on page 58 in Language and Literacy:

D Writing

2 Uses letter-like shapes, symbols, letters, and words to convey meaning.

First Grade

3 Recognizes and uses basic conventions of print.

First graders can recognize and use some mechanical and grammatical conventions of writing, including left-to-right, spacing between words, uppercase letters (first word in a sentence, names of people, "I," days of the week and months of the year), and periods and question marks. Many children this age can write in simple sentences that include a subject, verb, and object. Examples of how first graders demonstrate these skills include:

- using upper- and lowercase letters correctly when writing a science observation;
- re-reading a journal entry aloud, pausing correctly at the end of sentences, and adding missing periods;
- editing a story with a teacher's help and changing the first letter in the first words of each sentence to uppercase letters;
- writing questions to ask a guest speaker and putting question marks at the end of each question;
- writing simple, correctly-structured sentences describing a book about wolves.

Second Grade

3 Uses some mechanical and grammatical conventions.

Second graders often know more mechanical and grammatical conventions than they demonstrate in their day-to-day writing. When encouraged to apply what they know, or when writing final drafts, they can write legibly and use conventions such as periods, question marks, and exclamation marks; commas in a series; dates, greetings and closings of letters; and capitalization for the first word in a sentence, first and last names, "I," pronouns, and proper nouns. They often write in complete sentences and use nouns, verbs, and adjectives correctly. Examples include:

- using capitalization correctly when writing a "thank you" letter after a class trip to the railroad museum;
- placing an exclamation point in the opening line of a story and reading it aloud with emphasis;
- using commas to separate a list of adjectives in a story after noticing how this was done in a book;
- experimenting with quotation marks;
- reviewing a rough draft with a classmate and fixing capitals and periods.

Third Grade

3 Applies mechanical and grammatical conventions when drafting and editing.

Third graders can write legibly in script and use conventions such as endmarks, commas, capitalization, quotation marks for dialogue, apostrophes to indicate singular possession, and periods in abbreviations. They can use complete declarative and interrogative sentences, correct parts of speech, and principles of agreement (subject/verb, noun, pronoun). They can review their work independently for spelling, mechanics, and presentation. Examples include:

- using capitalization correctly when writing (for example, first and last names, first word in a sentence, the pronoun "I," proper nouns);
- re-reading a story and checking it for correct use of periods, question marks, exclamation points;
- using commas in a series, dates in greetings and closings of letters, and addresses;
- including dialogue in a story and applying quotation marks correctly;
- creating a final draft of a composition and including correct page format (for example, margins, indentations, paragraphs).

II Language and Literacy
D Writing

Preschool-3	Preschool-4	Kindergarten

Preschool-3

Not expected at this level.

Preschool-4

Not expected at this level.

Kindergarten

See the following indicator on page 58 in Language and Literacy:

D Writing

2 Uses letter-like shapes, symbols, letters, and words to convey meaning.

First Grade

4 Uses strategies to create invented and conventional spellings.

Using invented or temporary spellings is one way that first graders demonstrate their understanding of how to blend and segment letters and words. When children have extensive opportunities to use writing purposefully in the classroom, they begin to approximate conventional spellings more closely. With encouragement from teachers, first graders can spell correctly three- and four-letter short vowel words, words they studied previously, and words that follow consistent spelling patterns. Examples include:

- using initial consonants and letter-sound correspondence to more closely approximate conventional spellings;

- using resources from their environment (peers, personal dictionaries, labels in the classroom, word walls, charts, books) to help with spelling;

- recognizing the difference between invented spellings and conventional spellings in their own writing;

- using conventional spellings of high frequency words (for example, "and," "the," "they," "have");

- referring to their plans for the day as references for spelling words correctly when writing an end-of-day reflection.

Second Grade

4 Uses conventional spelling with increasing accuracy.

Second graders can be expected to spell correctly previously studied words, words that follow regular spelling patterns, and frequently used words. They can spell unfamiliar words representing all the phonemes with letters. They often rely on references (for example, word lists, dictionaries, charts) to help them spell accurately. Examples include:

- spelling high frequency words correctly on a regular basis;

- applying a spelling rule to guess how to write an unfamiliar word;

- referring to a word list in order to spell a word correctly;

- proofreading a homework assignment and correcting a few misspelled words;

- spelling words like "communication" as "comunicashun";

- figuring out the correct spelling of a word by using a children's dictionary, knowledge of alphabetical order, or by sounding out the word by syllables.

Third Grade

4 Uses a variety of spelling strategies.

By third grade, children should use standard spellings consistently for previously studied words and for words that follow regular patterns. They can apply their knowledge of phonics, root words, prefixes, suffixes, word families, and syllabication, and can spell an unfamiliar word representing each sound with letters. Examples include:

- using dictionaries or other references to help them spell accurately;

- sounding out a complex word by syllables and figuring it out correctly;

- noticing misspelled words and making corrections when reviewing drafts;

- using standard spellings in daily assignments (homework, math problems, science observations).

II Language and Literacy

II Language and Literacy

D Writing

Preschool-3	Preschool-4	Kindergarten
Not expected at this level.	Not expected at this level.	Not expected at this level.

First Grade

5 Reviews, shares, and makes simple changes in writing.

With encouragement to re-read their own writing, six year olds may realize they have misspelled a familiar word or omitted periods, capitals, or an important detail. They like to share their writing with a friend or with the class, and after some prompting from a teacher or peer, can make a simple change in their writing. Examples of emerging editing and revision skills include:

- re-reading a story, deciding there is a missing detail, and adding it;
- reading a story to a friend and then deciding to attach a new page in order to add another section;
- returning to a research report about bats after reading another book and learning something new;
- writing about a baseball game, looking over the story, then adding a few periods and capital letters;
- re-reading a story and recognizing that a sentence doesn't make sense;
- asking questions and giving comments to another student and, as a result, getting a new idea to add to their own story.

Second Grade

5 Clarifies or elaborates writing.

Seven year olds can improve and clarify their writing when given opportunities to share their writing and re-read it. They can rearrange words or sentences, adjust word choices, add details, and delete extraneous information. Some ways second graders demonstrate revision skills include:

- re-reading a story, deciding there is a missing detail, and adding it;
- deciding to change some simple sentences into compound sentences after a conference with the teacher;
- changing the ending of a story after sharing it with a friend or the class;
- deciding to include illustrations as part of a final draft of a report;
- adding supporting details to an expository piece.

Third Grade

5 Revises drafts to refine writing.

With some assistance from adults and peers, eight year olds can recognize when they have left out some important details or included too many. They know how to add more descriptive language, rewrite sentences to create greater clarity, or vary sentence structure to make their writing more interesting. Some ways third graders demonstrate revision skills include:

- reading a story to a peer and talking about whether to add or remove some information;
- sharing a story with the class and deciding to change the beginning or ending;
- after writing for a while, reflecting on the topic, realizing it is too broad, narrowing it down, and eliminating some text;
- deciding that all of the sentences begin the same way and rearranging some phrases;
- discussing ways that a classmate might change a part of his or her writing to make it more persuasive.

❚❚ Language and Literacy

E   Research

Preschool-3

Not expected at this level.

Preschool-4

Not expected at this level.

Kindergarten

Not expected at this level.

First Grade

See the following indicator on page 19 in Personal and Social Development:

C Approaches to learning

4 Begins to use technology to assist with thinking and problem-solving.

See the following indicator on page 43 in Language and Literacy:

C Reading

1 Shows interest in books and reading.

See the following indicator on page 51 in Language and Literacy:

C Reading

5 Comprehends and interprets fiction and non-fiction text.

See the following indicator on page 61 in Language and Literacy:

D Writing

2 Writes for different purposes.

Second Grade

See the following indicator on page 19 in Personal and Social Development:

C Approaches to learning

4 Uses technology to assist with thinking and problem-solving.

See the following indicator on page 53 in Language and Literacy:

C Reading

5 Reads for varied purposes.

See the following indicator on page 61 in Language and Literacy:

D Writing

2 Writes for different purposes in different formats.

Third Grade

1 **Gathers and uses information for research purposes.**

By third grade, children can be expected to follow a set of directions, a model, or a rubric to carry out a basic research project. They can use strategies to identify topics (for example, brainstorming or webbing), gather information from a few sources, and take notes about essential ideas. They can use reference information (for example, table of contents, indices, charts, illustrations) to locate answers to their questions. After conferencing with an adult, they can organize their work into a written report. Examples include:

- gathering information on the Internet about a topic and taking notes;
- using encyclopedias, biographies, and CD-ROMs to obtain facts about a topic;
- organizing research information with a web or other graphic organizer;
- including charts and illustrations in the final draft of a research report;
- collaborating with a classmate on a research project and brainstorming questions about the topic before beginning the research.

Mathematical Thinking

The focus in this domain is on children's approaches to mathematical thinking and problem-solving. Emphasis is placed on how students acquire and use strategies to perceive, understand, and solve mathematical problems. Mathematics is about patterns and relationships, and about seeking multiple solutions to problems. In this domain, the content of mathematics (concepts and procedures) is stressed, but the larger context of understanding and application (knowing and doing) is also of great importance.

III Mathematical Thinking
A Mathematical processes

Preschool-3

1 Shows interest in solving mathematical problems.

Three year olds are drawn into the world of mathematics in many ways. They observe people counting money, measuring things, and talking about two shoes and two eyes. Adults frequently ask them how old they are. Three year olds show their beginning understanding of mathematical thinking by:

- talking about who has more cookies or more play dough;
- sorting the counting bears by color;
- deciding that square blocks belong in the empty space on the block shelf because their shape matches the picture;
- responding to questions about the number of eyes, ears, or hands they have;
- noticing a pattern on another child's coat or around a bulletin board;
- holding up three fingers when asked how old they are;
- using number words in their play;
- drawing many circles and talking about them;
- talking about "lots and lots—millions—of people at the store today."

Preschool-4

1 Begins to use simple strategies to solve mathematical problems.

Four year olds encounter real life mathematical problems throughout the day: How many cartons of milk do we need for snack? How can I fit these boxes together? How many days until we go to the zoo? With guidance, and in a classroom environment that supports asking questions, preschoolers can begin to solve simple mathematical problems in concrete ways, and offer basic explanations for their solutions. Examples include:

- asking a friend if there are "more people in your house or in mine?";
- trying to find a way to keep building a house with blocks, even though the long rectangular blocks have all been used;
- asking a friend for a particular pattern block to complete a design;
- figuring out how many small cups it takes to fill the pitcher at the water table;
- wondering aloud how they can make their balls of play dough into a snake as long as the teacher's;
- deciding who is older if one child is 4 and another is 4½.

Kindergarten

1 Begins to use and explain strategies to solve mathematical problems.

Solving real-life problems helps children make connections among the math they are learning at school, other parts of their lives, and other types of learning. Problem-solving involves posing questions, trying different strategies, and explaining one's thinking by stating reasons a particular strategy worked. Young children solve problems and explain their reasoning by working with concrete objects, drawing pictures, or acting out solutions. They show this emerging skill by:

- asking questions to clarify problems (for example, "Will the new rabbit cage be big enough for all the baby bunnies?");
- saying, "I gave Sammy one of my cookies because I had three and he had one. Now we have the same, two and two!";
- estimating whether there are enough blocks to build a road from here to there, and then testing the guess by building the road;
- solving problems by guessing and checking (for example, figuring out how many apples are needed for snack if each child is served half an apple).

First Grade

1 Applies concepts and strategies to solve mathematical problems.

With guidance, first graders can begin to set up a problem, determine the tools and materials needed to solve it, and apply strategies (such as trial and error, looking for a pattern, making a drawing, "counting on" or backwards, or counting in groups) to find solutions. When asked, they can discuss the effectiveness of their strategies and explain their reasoning. Examples include:

- using trial and error to figure out how many unifix cubes it takes to balance a scale;

- figuring out how many additional books are needed for the class if there are only 12 books and 21 children in the class;

- using a calculator to determine the amount of money collected at the end of a bake sale if 100 cookies are sold at 25¢ each;

- using a drawing to find the total number of wheels on three bicycles and two cars;

- counting by fives using tally marks to determine the favorite name for the class pet;

- using unifix cubes in sets of ten and "counting on" to determine the total number of children in all of the first grades.

Second Grade

1 Applies concepts and strategies to solve mathematical problems.

Second graders can approach problem-solving by making plans and carrying them out. With encouragement, they can try more than one approach and reflect on whether their strategies and solutions are reasonable. Seven year olds like to invent methods for solving problems as well as draw on ones they have learned (including trial and error, noticing patterns, making a drawing, using tools or technology). Examples include:

- finding hidden shapes embedded in a complex design by systematically moving from one part of the design to the next and listing the shapes located;

- making drawings to figure out the solution to a problem (for example, how many legs do three horses and four chickens have?);

- using a calculator and a calendar to determine the number of days in a year after estimating the answer;

- making an organized list to figure out how many different outfits can be made with two pairs of pants and three shirts.

Third Grade

1 Applies concepts and strategies to solve mathematical problems.

Third graders can approach a problem systematically by making a plan, carrying it out, and evaluating its effectiveness. They can apply a variety of strategies, including trial and error, guessing and checking, making drawings, diagrams, or charts, using mental math, using technology, and making an organized list or table. Third graders demonstrate problem-solving skills by:

- applying a successful strategy used with one problem to a more complex problem;

- breaking a complex problem into simpler parts;

- making a drawing to figure out different ways of combining members of the class into even teams;

- making a chart or table (for example, to keep track of how many times a six is rolled in 30 rolls of a die);

- checking an estimate by using a calculator;

- using a graphics program on the computer to create a scale drawing for the class model.

Preschool-3

See the following indicator on page 72 in Mathematical Thinking:

A Mathematical processes

1 Shows interest in solving mathematical problems.

See the following indicator on page 40 in Language and Literacy:

B Speaking

2 Uses expanded vocabulary and language for a variety of purposes.

Preschool-4

See the following indicator on page 72 in Mathematical Thinking:

A Mathematical processes

1 Shows interest in solving mathematical problems.

See the following indicator on page 40 in Language and Literacy:

B Speaking

2 Uses expanded vocabulary and language for a variety of purposes.

Kindergarten

2 Uses words and representations to describe mathematical ideas.

School provides kindergarten children with many opportunities to communicate mathematical ideas. When teachers ask children to describe how they know the number of crackers needed at the snack table, they encourage children to attach language to mathematical thinking. Five year olds represent their thinking by using objects, fingers, drawings, bodies, and occasionally, symbols. These representations help children retain information and allow children to reflect on their own problem-solving strategies. Examples include:

- explaining that they chose a puzzle piece because its shape matched the other shape;
- telling a friend or teacher how they built the tallest block structure in the school;
- drawing a picture of a Lego structure they made so they can rebuild it the next day;
- explaining that they put all the long sticks in one box and all the short sticks in another box;
- asking for a bigger container at the sand table because they want to make a larger building or move more sand.

First Grade

2 Communicates and represents mathematical thinking.

For first graders, discussion, representation, reading, and writing are essential to mathematical thinking. They can explain their reasoning, clarify their ideas, and represent their thinking using words and pictures. Some ways they do this include:

- sorting a group of objects and then explaining the sorting rule;

- justifying their reasoning for solving a problem by applying a strategy used to solve a similar problem;

- drawing a picture to represent and model a problem or situation, solving it, and then explaining the process;

- reading a simple word problem, interpreting it, and writing a number sentence to find the solution;

- listening to a peer's explanation of how a problem was solved and suggesting an alternate approach;

- using mathematical terms to describe a situation accurately (for example, "more," "not as much," or "about the same" to describe quantities).

Second Grade

2 Communicates and represents mathematical thinking.

For second graders, discussion, representation, reading, and writing help them organize and clarify their thinking. They can create and use representations to organize, record, and communicate mathematical ideas. They can describe and justify their reasoning using mathematical language, numbers, and pictures. Examples include:

- describing the strategy used to estimate the number of buttons in a jar and how the actual answer was derived;

- connecting number words and numerals to the numbers they represent (for example, reading the number 562 and knowing how to write it as five hundred sixty-two);

- using shapes to represent objects on a map of the classroom and creating a key to explain the map;

- explaining a pattern shown on the class weather chart;

- using the decimal notation for dollars and cents (for example, writing $1.25);

- listening to a classmate explain how he solved a problem and questioning the reasoning he used;

- using ordinal numbers to describe objects or events by their positions (for example, seventh, twenty-first).

Third Grade

2 Communicates and represents mathematical thinking.

Third graders can use logic, reasoning, and the language of mathematics to explain and represent their thinking. In math journals and class discussions, they use pictures, symbols, and words to describe their thinking and justify their approaches and solutions. Examples include:

- participating in math discussions (for example, describing solutions to math puzzles and games);

- linking mathematical language to symbols (for example, describing three quarters of something and writing it as ¾ or saying that two numbers are unequal and using the symbol ≠ ;

- explaining addition and subtraction problems using pictures, words, symbols and algorithms;

- using words to explain mathematical observations (for example, after doing a series of division problems, explaining that when a number is divided by a smaller number, the result will be smaller than the original number);

- representing amounts of money using decimals;

- using Roman numerals I, V, X, L, and C correctly.

Preschool-3

1 Shows curiosity and interest in counting and numbers.

Most three year olds are interested in numbers and counting. They may ask, "How many?" and begin to say numbers in order, counting verbally up to three, six, or even ten with help. They can count small sets of one, two, or three objects with one-to-one correspondence. Most three year olds can identify a group of one, two, or three objects without counting, visually recognize whether two sets have the same or one has more, and make sets of up to three items. Examples include:

• following directions for getting "just two jars of paint" for the easel;

• recognizing that they have the same number of cars as a friend does;

• counting out loud to themselves while occupied at an activity;

• commenting that there are two cookies left on the plate without counting;

• being actively involved in reading a counting book;

• commenting that everyone at snack has two crackers and one cup of juice;

• singing counting songs and enjoying fingerplays about counting.

Preschool-4

1 Shows beginning understanding of number and quantity.

Four year olds can count five to ten objects meaningfully using one-to-one correspondence, and some can count verbally up to 20 or 30. Most four year olds understand that the last number named in the collection represents the last object as well as the total number of objects. They are just learning that the next number in the counting sequence is one more than the number just named and continue to explore the meaning of "more" and "less." Examples include:

• pointing to each object they count and assigning the appropriate number to it;

• recognizing that there are four blocks without counting them;

• commenting that there are more cars than tow trucks in the block area;

• telling a friend who is first in line, "I am second";

• adding a friend's two yellow beads to their own two yellow beads and saying, "I have four beads";

• filling in the next number when the teacher says "4, 5, 6, ...";

• counting footsteps, jumps, or repetitions of exercises.

Kindergarten

1 Shows understanding of number and quantity.

Kindergarten children can count objects to at least 20; many learn to count verbally (that is, by rote) to 100. They can count using one-to-one correspondence reliably, use objects to represent numbers, and use numerals to represent quantities. With experience, they can begin to understand that a set of objects equals the same number regardless of the position, shape, or order of the objects. They continue to learn about ordinal numbers (first through tenth) and understand that the last number named in a collection represents not only the last object, but the total number of objects as well. Examples include:

• explaining that there are 17 people at the circle today, after counting them aloud with their classmates;

• associating the correct numeral with sets of up to ten objects;

• using number words to show understanding of the common numerical property among nine children, nine cups, nine trucks, and nine blocks;

• continuing counting pennies to ten after a friend stopped at 6 (. . . "7, 8, 9, 10").

First Grade

1 Shows understanding of number and quantity.

Six year olds can count, read, model, and write whole numbers to 100 or more. It is essential that first graders understand that numbers can be represented in many ways (for example, 10, ten, two sets of five stars). Their understanding of number includes knowing the value of coins. Examples of how six year olds demonstrate their understanding include:

- looking at a set of six objects and instantly recognizing it as six;

- recognizing equivalent forms of the same number (for example, knowing that 30 is the same quantity if it is 30 horses or 30 M&Ms or 15+15 red dots);

- counting the number of objects in a group with understanding and writing the correct numeral to describe the set (for example, writing the numeral 30 to match 30 cubes);

- looking at a set of coins and identifying the value of each coin.

Second Grade

1 Shows understanding of number, quantities, and their relationships.

Seven year olds can count, read, write, model, order, and compare whole numbers to at least 999. They can express quantities in different ways (for example, 30 as 15 + 15 or 3 tens) and they can group numbers into hundreds, tens, and ones, identifying the place value for each digit. Their understanding of quantity includes modeling, representing, and solving problems involving money (pennies, nickels, dimes, quarters, and dollar bills). They demonstrate their understanding by:

- reading and writing two- and three-digit numerals purposefully, such as recording card game scores;

- describing the comparative relationship of numbers using the symbols >, <, = (for example, 234 > 150);

- counting by 3s and 4s to 100 and by 10s or in multiples of 10s beginning at different numbers (for example, from 20, 55, or 120);

- switching among different counts (for example 100, 200, 300, 310, 320, 330, 331, 332, 333, etc.);

- identifying the value of a group of coins (5 dimes, 3 nickels, and 3 pennies equal 68¢).

Third Grade

1 Shows understanding of number, quantities, and their relationships.

By third grade, students demonstrate their comprehension of the meaning of four- and five-digit whole numbers by modeling, ordering, and comparing numbers to at least 10,000. They show understanding of place value by calculating addition and subtraction algorithms accurately, using models to explain place value, and representing four- and five-digit numbers using expanded notation. They begin to explore numbers less than zero using a number line. Examples include:

- ordering numbers by relative size (640 comes before 1200 because it is smaller by about half);

- representing comparisons of large numbers or quantities using equations with the symbols <, >, =, ≠;

- rounding numbers to the nearest ten, hundred, and thousand when solving problems where an approximate answer is sufficient;

- representing a five-digit number in different ways (5,432 is the same as five thousands, four hundreds, three tens, and two ones, or 5000 + 400 + 30 + 2).

Preschool-3

See the following indicator on page 76 in Mathematical Thinking:

B   Number and operations

1   Shows curiosity and interest in counting and numbers.

Preschool-4

See the following indicator on page 76 in Mathematical Thinking:

B   Number and operations

1   Shows beginning understanding of number and quantity.

Kindergarten

2   Begins to understand relationships between quantities.

Five year olds begin to explore the relationships of one quantity to another. They can compare two sets with up to 10 objects and use such vocabulary as "more," "less," "equal," or "the same number as" to describe them. They are beginning to understand how quantity changes when they combine sets to make larger ones or decrease the size of sets by removing items. Some kindergartners begin to make realistic guesses about small quantities and show initial awareness of fractional parts (halves, quarters) using concrete objects. Examples include:

* investigating strategies for creating different quantities (for example, by working with red and blue cubes to learn that seven can be made up of two red cubes and five blue cubes or three blue cubes and four red cubes, etc.);

* recognizing that five large objects are the same as five small objects in terms of number;

* knowing that five is closer to one than it is to 20;

* agreeing to share cookies with a friend and commenting, "I have half of a sugar cookie and half of a peanut butter cookie."

First Grade

2 Shows understanding of relationships among quantities.

First graders' understanding of quantity includes comparing numbers to 100 and ordering numbers to at least 20. Work with concrete materials (blocks, Popsicle sticks, trading games) helps them to grasp the concept of grouping by tens and place value. They can combine and break apart numbers, identify odd and even numbers, and describe the relative position and magnitude of whole numbers (for example, finding 40 on a number line and explaining that it is 10 less than 50). First graders can understand and represent simple fractions (¼, ⅓, ½). Examples include:

- comparing two or more sets and determining which is more, less, or equal to and using symbols (<, >, =) and words to describe the comparisons;

- composing or decomposing numbers (3 tens and 2 ones is the same as 32 or 32 is the same as 3 tens and 2 ones);

- comparing ½ of a pizza with ¼ of a pizza and explaining why ¼ is less than ½;

- identifying positions 1st to 20th (for example, when lining up to go outside);

- comparing a quarter to 25 pennies and explaining why they are equal.

Second Grade

See the following indicator on page 77 in Mathematical Thinking:

B Number and operations

1 Shows understanding of number, quantities and their relationships.

Third Grade

See the following indicator on page 77 in Mathematical Thinking:

B Number and operations

1 Shows understanding of number, quantities and their relationships.

▥ Mathematical Thinking

B   Number and operations

Preschool-3	Preschool-4	Kindergarten

Preschool-3

Not expected at this level.

Preschool-4

Not expected at this level.

Kindergarten

See the following indicator on page 78 in Mathematical Thinking:

B Number and operations

2 Begins to understand relationships between quantities.

First Grade

3 **Uses addition and subtraction to solve problems with one- and two-digit numbers.**

First graders recognize and use the symbols "+" and "-" in equations, combine and separate sets, and understand that addition and subtraction are inverse operations. Some strategies used for combining and separating quantities include: counting on fingers, doubling (for example, 4 + 4, 5 + 5), and knowing "number families" (if 2 + 8 = 10, then 8 + 2 is also 10). As they acquire facility with strategies for finding sums and differences with numbers up to 20, they begin to apply these same strategies with numbers to 100. Examples include:

- explaining that 5 - ? = 2 is the same as ? + 2 = 5;

- figuring out sums in a dice game using doubles or doubles + 1 (if 5 + 5 = 10, then 5 + 6 is one more than 10);

- counting on from 10 (for example, given a group of 10 and asked to add three more objects, the child counts on from 10 instead of beginning at 1);

- finding the missing number in addition and subtraction number sentences when the missing number is 10 or less.

Second Grade

2 **Understands and uses addition and subtraction to solve problems with two- and three-digit numbers.**

By second grade, students understand the inverse relationship between addition and subtraction (3 + 4 = 7 and 7 - 4 = 3) and can add and subtract two- and three-digit numbers. Knowing number facts and "number families" (2 + 8 = 10, but 3 + 7 is also 10) to 20 and using strategies (such as counting on, counting backwards, counting in groups, and doubling) is essential for second graders' fluency in finding solutions to problems involving larger numbers. They can use regrouping with at least two-digit numbers. Examples include:

- calculating scores in card games using doubles and doubles plus one (for example, 6 + 7 = 13 because 7 + 7 = 14, and 6 + 7 is one less than 14);

- relying on knowledge of number family relationships when figuring out a solution to a problem (if 9 - 3 = 6, then I'll have 60¢ left if I start with 90¢ and buy a 30¢ sticker);

- finding the difference between two scores in a game ("Your score was 250 and mine was 180, so you won by 70.").

Third Grade

2 **Estimates and accurately computes addition and subtraction problems.**

Third graders apply strategies they know for adding and subtracting numbers to 100 as they work with larger numbers up to 10,000. They set up algorithms and select appropriate methods and tools to solve problems. They can make reasonable estimates of quantities, time, money, and measurements, and know how to check the accuracy of their answers. Examples of how they apply these strategies include:

- mentally calculating the total weight of a group of objects by breaking down and combining numbers (for example, 123 lbs. + 114 lbs. = 200 + 23 + 10 + 4, or 237 lbs.);

- using addition and subtraction algorithms accurately in everyday problem-solving situations;

- using front-end techniques to estimate an answer (3457 + 5331 + 132 is at least 3 thousands + 5 thousands or 8000);

- using strategies such as rounding off to estimate an approximate answer;

- estimating the value of a collection of bills and coins and then using a calculator to determine the exact value.

III Mathematical Thinking

B Number and operations

Preschool-3

Not expected at this level.

Preschool-4

Not expected at this level.

Kindergarten

See the following indicator on page 72 in Mathematical Thinking:

A Mathematical processes

1 Begins to use and explain strategies to solve mathematical problems.

See the following indicator on page 78 in Mathematical Thinking:

B Number and operations

2 Begins to understand relationships between quantities.

See the following indicator on page 100 in Mathematical Thinking:

E Measurement

2 Explores common instruments for measuring during work and play.

First Grade

4 Makes reasonable estimates of quantities and checks for accuracy.

Through estimation activities, first graders extend their understanding of number. They can make realistic guesses using words and phrases such as "smaller than," "bigger than," "same," and "almost" with sets to about 100 objects. Some examples of this skill include:

- looking at a group of objects and deciding if it is more than 10, about 20, or less than 50;
- estimating the number of objects in a group, explaining the reasoning behind the estimate, and then checking the estimate by counting;
- estimating the total number of children in the first grade and then checking the estimate using a calculator;
- explaining that 21 + 36 + 2 is at least 2 tens + 3 tens or 50;
- pointing to the approximate location of the number 45 on a multiples of 10 number line and explaining why it is between 40 and 50;
- showing a beginning understanding of large numbers ("There are over a hundred children in the school.");
- dividing a pile of M&Ms in half and then counting to check for accuracy.

Second Grade

3 Makes reasonable estimates of quantities and checks for accuracy.

As second graders develop estimation skills, they come to understand that mathematics is not always about being exact. For second graders, understanding estimation includes making realistic guesses using such phrases as "near," "about," "close to," "more than," "greater than," and "less than." They can check the reasonableness of their answers. Examples include:

- looking at some objects and making a thoughtful guess about the amount that comes close to the actual quantity (estimating that there are about 58 cubes in a jar that actually contains 50 cubes);
- showing an understanding of large numbers by estimating quantity (saying that about 75 children eat in the lunch room each day, or that there are more than 300 children in the school);
- rounding numbers to the nearest ten to find approximate answers;
- using a front-end strategy with 3- or 4-digit numbers (563 + 222 + 87 is at least 5 hundreds + 2 hundreds or 700);
- describing the set of cubes in their hand as "about ⅓" of the entire box of cubes.

Third Grade

See the following indicator on page 81 in Mathematical Thinking:

B Number and operations

2 Estimates and accurately computes addition and subtraction problems.

III Mathematical Thinking
B   Number and operations

Preschool-3

Not expected at this level.

Preschool-4

Not expected at this level.

Kindergarten

Not expected at this level.

First Grade

See the following indicator on page 79 in Mathematical Thinking:

B Number and operations

2 Shows understanding of relationships among quantities.

See the following indicator on page 83 in Mathematical Thinking:

B Number and operations

4 Makes reasonable estimates of quantities and checks for accuracy.

Second Grade

4 **Demonstrates beginning understanding of multiplication and division.**

In second grade, children multiply by doing repeated addition, arranging quantities in arrays, and counting by multiples. They are beginning to learn their times tables, especially 2s, 5s, and 10s. They explore division as "sharing," and in this way learn about dividing units into equal parts and sometimes having a remainder. They can identify and represent fractions including halves, quarters, thirds, eighths, and sixths. Examples include:

- creating a picture that shows three rows of five plants to solve a problem about how to plant 15 plants in even rows;

- using repeated addition (7 + 7 + 7 + 7) to determine how many players there are on four teams of seven players each;

- dividing a deck of cards by giving each of four children one card at a time, going around in a circle until all the cards are distributed, and then counting how many cards each person holds in order to solve the problem 52 ÷ 4;

- representing the portion of pizza that was eaten as ⅜;

- dividing objects into equal parts (cutting an apple into four equal parts).

Third Grade

3 **Uses some strategies to multiply and divide whole numbers.**

Third graders who understand the meaning of multiplication and division know that multiplication is repeated addition, division is repeated subtraction, and that these are inverse operations. They apply memorized number facts to multiply accurately a multi-digit number by a one-digit number and divide a multi-digit number by a one-digit number. Some examples of their fluency with multiplication and division strategies are:

- seeing the relationship between repeated addition and multiplication (7 x 4 = 28 or 7 + 7 + 7 + 7);

- counting in multiples to solve a practical problem (calculating how many cookies are in six packages of four cookies each by counting by 4s);

- explaining the special properties of "0" and "1" when multiplying and dividing numbers;

- using algorithms to determine products and quotients when solving problems in everyday situations ("How many students can go on the field trip if each bus holds 75 students and there are 6 buses?").

III Mathematical Thinking

III Mathematical Thinking

B Number and operations

Preschool-3

Not expected at this level.

Preschool-4

Not expected at this level.

Kindergarten

See the following indicator on page 78 in Mathematical Thinking:

B Number and operations

2 Begins to understand relationships between quantities.

First Grade

See the following indicator on page 79 in Mathematical Thinking:

B Number and operations

2 Shows beginning understanding of relationships among quantities.

See the following indicator on page 83 in Mathematical Thinking:

B Number and operations

4 Makes reasonable estimates of quantities and checks for accuracy.

Second Grade

See the following indicator on page 85 in Mathematical Thinking:

B Number and operations

4 Demonstrates beginning understanding of multiplication and division.

Third Grade

4 **Shows understanding of fractions and decimals as parts of wholes.**

Third graders can use concrete materials (pattern blocks, Cuisenaire rods, geoboards) to demonstrate their understanding of fractional relationships. With objects and numbers, they can identify and interpret fractions as parts of wholes. They can begin to add and subtract commonly-used fractions. They are beginning to explore commonly-used decimals, especially in relationship to money. Examples of these skills include:

- using common fractions, decimals, and percentages (for example, identifying 25%, .25, ¼ all as one quarter of a whole or writing a half-dollar as 50¢ or $.50);

- dividing real objects into equal parts in a variety of ways and describing and comparing their relative sizes (for example, cutting an apple into four parts, two parts, or eight parts and describing and comparing the size differences);

- dividing sets into fractional parts (separating 24 M&Ms into three equal piles in order to find ⅓ of the total);

- adding and subtracting fractions (for example, ½ - ¼ = ¼).

III Mathematical Thinking

Preschool-3

1 Sorts objects into subgroups that vary by one attribute.

Three year olds are intrigued and fascinated with their emerging ability to order their environment. As they begin to see how objects can be grouped together by single attributes or characteristics, they gain a sense of control in a new arena. They show their ability to construct order by:

- looking at the children at the table and sorting them ("Some of these people are boys and some of these people are girls.");
- picking out all the red crayons from the box and announcing, "This is how many red crayons we have";
- selecting all the big buttons and putting them in one box, then picking out all the small buttons and putting them in another box;
- putting the plastic food in a cupboard and the dress-up clothes on hooks in the dramatic play area;
- noticing a common attribute and commenting on it ("These are all round.").

Preschool-4

1 Sorts objects into subgroups that vary by one or two attributes.

Children this age enjoy sorting and classifying because these activities help them gain control of their world by ordering it. After learning to sort objects by one attribute, some four year olds begin to sort by two attributes (for example, putting all the big circles here, the big triangles there, and the small circles here). Sorting and classifying introduce children to the order of mathematical thinking. As they play, children show their emerging understanding of order by:

- sorting the pegs according to color;
- sorting all the Lotto cards into piles of people and piles of animals;
- putting all the markers in one box and all the pencils in another box;
- sorting the buttons, beads, or pegs into egg cartons, with each compartment holding a different color or size;
- describing a group of objects according to a common attribute;
- sorting pattern blocks according to shape and color.

Kindergarten

1 Sorts objects into subgroups, classifying and comparing according to a rule.

Sorting objects into groups according to attributes is an important mathematical skill that requires children to recognize similarities among objects. Although some five year olds can only perceive one attribute at a time, most are able to integrate several attributes, such as sorting by color and size. Examples of skills in sorting and comparing include:

- sorting all the pegs or counting bears into groups by a single attribute such as size (long and short, or big and little) or color;
- sorting through a box of buttons and making up their own rules of organization (for example, "These are all rough and these are all smooth." or "These have two holes and these have four holes.");
- sorting the buttons by color, and then sorting each color group into large and small;
- sorting through Lotto cards and putting wild animals in one pile and farm animals in another;
- noticing that these pattern blocks have six sides and are yellow, and those blocks have three sides and are red.

First Grade

1 Sorts, classifies, and orders objects on the basis of several attributes.

Six year olds can sort, classify, and order objects by size, shape, color, function, number, and many other properties. They can describe their sorting rules and compare objects for similarities and differences. Ways children demonstrate these skills include:

- sorting a collection of keys into two groups: those with ridges on one side and those with ridges on both sides;

- describing similarities and differences among the shapes and sizes of seeds;

- comparing objects within a collection and putting the objects in order by size (for example, small to large, long to short);

- using sorting and classifying in social studies or science activities (organizing a list of neighborhood stores into three groups: ones that sell only food, ones that do not sell food, and ones that sell both food and other items);

- sorting a collection of objects according to their own sorting rule and having a partner guess the rule.

Second Grade

1 Sorts, classifies, and compares objects using attributes and quantities.

Second graders can sort objects and describe the rules they used, sort by a specific attribute, and compare objects for similarities and differences. They can compare quantities to determine if they are equal or if one is more or less than another, as well as order groups using the names of ordinal numbers. Ways children demonstrate sorting skills include:

- sorting math materials by several attributes (for example, dividing shapes into a group of large plastic ones and small wooden ones);

- describing an example of intersecting sets (for example, separating shoes into those with laces and those without, but noting that both groups contain leather shoes);

- counting two sets of buttons to determine which has more;

- using classifying and ordering in social studies or science activities (lining up a group of plant seedlings in order by size or arranging countries by those that speak English, Spanish, or French);

- ordering a collection of objects by weight from lightest to heaviest.

Third Grade

See the following indicator on page 91 in Mathematical Thinking:

C Patterns, relationships, and functions

1 Uses the concept of patterning to make predictions and draw conclusions.

See the following indicator on page 119 in Scientific Thinking:

B Physical science

1 Identifies, describes, and compares properties, positions, and motion of objects.

III Mathematical Thinking

C Patterns, relationships, and functions

Preschool-3

Not expected at this level.

Preschool-4

2 Recognizes simple patterns and duplicates them.

Like sorting and classifying, recognizing and creating patterns also introduce children to the concept of order in the world. Four year olds' natural curiosity can be directed toward recognition of patterns. They can copy simple patterns with sounds and objects. Children show their recognition of patterns by:

- copying a sound pattern of two claps and a pause, then one clap and a pause;
- seeing the *"o x o x"* shapes on a border and copying the pattern with crayons;
- drawing dots on a paper in a repeating pattern (for example, green, blue, green, blue);
- recognizing the pattern in a predictable book and saying the next line before turning the page;
- predicting the next item in a simple AB pattern;
- stringing beads in a repeating pattern according to color, shape, or size;
- commenting that several children are wearing red shirts;
- making a pattern while finger painting.

Kindergarten

2 Recognizes, duplicates, and extends patterns.

Patterns are a critical component of the foundation of mathematical thinking. Five year olds can recognize, create, copy, and extend simple patterns using concrete objects, sounds, and physical movements. They can describe a pattern, recognize patterns in the environment, and use a pattern to predict what comes next. Many kindergartners can begin to use letters and numbers to describe an existing pattern (an ABA pattern is the same as a 121 pattern) and recognize patterns in a counting sequence (2, 4, 6, 8). They begin to understand patterns by:

- seeing the pattern in a string of beads and determining which bead is needed to continue the pattern;
- duplicating a pattern of clapping (for example, two fast claps and a pause, then two slow claps and a pause);
- recognizing and describing a pattern in the classroom environment (for example, in the border around a bulletin board, on a T-shirt, or on wallpaper samples);
- knowing that a red-red-green/red-red-green pattern is the same as a clap-clap-step/clap-clap-step pattern.

First Grade

2 Makes, copies, and extends patterns.

Patterns are a critical part of mathematical thinking. By six, children can identify the unit of pattern (AAB; □+2); create and extend patterns concretely, symbolically, and numerically; and describe and analyze them. They can recognize patterns in the environment, in literature, and with numbers. With encouragement, they can begin to use patterns to make predictions. Examples include:

- making, copying, and extending a pattern with their voice, body, and musical instruments;
- identifying the rule needed to extend a pattern or determine a missing element in a pattern (for example, □ + 3 = Δ; jump, hop, step, ___, hop, step);
- transferring a pattern from one medium to another (for example, making an AAB pattern with color cubes and then clapping the pattern);
- recognizing the patterns of 10 on the calendar;
- recognizing a pattern in a book and making a prediction about what will come next;
- creating a number pattern and explaining the rule.

Second Grade

2 Makes, copies, and extends patterns with actions, objects, words, and numbers.

Second graders can recognize, create, and describe patterns in a variety of formats (for example, visually and auditorally, concretely and pictorially, and with numbers, both linearly and in a matrix). They can identify and extend patterns in numbers (for example, even and odd numbers). Examples include:

- creating multiple representations of the same pattern (for example, first with pattern blocks, then with cut-out representations, and finally as a drawing);
- identifying the rule needed to extend a pattern or determine a missing element in a pattern (15, 13, 11, ___, 7, 5);
- recognizing patterns in calendars, daily schedules, and in games (such as winning moves in tic-tac-toe);
- describing how a repeating number pattern is generated in order to predict an answer to a problem;
- identifying a pattern in a list of related numbers and extending the list (1 bike = 2 wheels, 2 bikes = 4 wheels, etc.);
- using a calculator to make a number pattern with large numbers.

Third Grade

1 Uses the concept of patterning to make predictions and draw conclusions.

Third graders create, extend, and describe patterns with actions, objects, and numbers. By this age, students apply their understanding of patterns to make predictions, draw conclusions, make generalizations, and solve problems (for example, adding or subtracting a constant number to or from a series of numbers, noticing the pattern, and predicting the next number). Examples include:

- creating an intricate drawing of a geometric pattern on paper and reproducing it with another material (for example, drawing the pattern on paper and reproducing it as a weaving);
- identifying the rule needed to extend a pattern or determine a missing element in a pattern (for example, 109, 99, 89, 79, ...);
- predicting the next numbers in a number pattern and then using a calculator to check accuracy;
- finding the dates for all the Tuesdays in a given year;
- figuring out how many yellow hexagons would be needed to complete the entire design, given the unit of pattern in one row of a pattern block design.

III Mathematical Thinking

Preschool-3

Not expected at this level.

Preschool-4

Not expected at this level.

Kindergarten

See the following indicator on page 76 in Mathematical Thinking:

B   Number and operations

1   Shows understanding of number and quantity.

See the following indicator on page 78 in Mathematical Thinking:

B   Number and operations

2   Begins to understand relationships between quantities.

First Grade

See the following indicator on page 77 in Mathematical Thinking:

B Number and operations

1 Shows understanding of number and quantity.

See the following indicator on page 79 in Mathematical Thinking:

B Number and operations

2 Shows beginning understanding of relationships among quantities.

Second Grade

3 **Expresses number relationships using equations and inequalities.**

Second graders can solve number sentences with equalities and inequalities where a number is missing and is represented by a letter or a geometric shape (for example, $10 - \Delta = 6$ or $7 > 2 + \Delta$). They can read and interpret real-world addition and subtraction problems with one unknown by constructing an equation and then using concrete objects, paper and pencil, or mental math to find the solution. Examples of this kind of algebraic thinking include:

- reading the problem, "There are 12 striped and spotted balls in all. Five have stripes. How many balls have spots?" and then creating the equation $5 + ? = 12$ to find the solution;

- generating a list of answers for the equation $8 > ? + 1$;

- labeling number sentences as true or false;

- identifying the pattern and finding the solution to the problem, "If there are four wheels on one car, how many wheels will there be on two cars?, three cars?, or four cars?"

Third Grade

2 **Uses variables in equations and inequalities to express number relationships.**

Third graders can express mathematical relationships using equations and inequalities where an unknown quantity is represented by a symbol or variable. They can read and interpret real-world problems with one unknown by constructing an equation and use concrete objects, paper and pencil, or mental math to find the solutions. As they investigate different types of equations, they develop an understanding of the mathematical properties of commutativity and associativity. Examples of how third graders explore relationships and functions (algebraic thinking) include:

- applying and explaining the rule to complete a table or chart ($\Delta \times 5 = \square$);

- creating a word problem for a given number sentence (for example, $22 \times 3 = ?$);

- explaining that a way to add $23 + 12$ mentally is to do $20 + 10 + 3 + 2$;

- identifying the correct operational symbol to make an equation true (for example, $3 \underline{?} 7 = 21$ and placing the "x" sign in the blank).

III Mathematical Thinking

III Mathematical Thinking

D Geometry and spatial relations

Preschool-3

1 Identifies several shapes.

Three year olds become aware of shapes in their world when they are taught to identify geometric shapes that have been labeled by the teacher. Although they focus initially on circles, they can be expected to match and identify squares and triangles as well. They begin to look at common objects with a new focus and gain mastery when encouraged to observe, explore, and name various shapes. They demonstrate this new skill by:

- becoming excited when they see letters on a page and can recognize that this one is a circle and that one looks like a cross;

- matching paper circles and triangles on the collage table with other circles and triangles;

- cleaning up the wooden blocks and placing them on the correct shelf by matching the shape of the block to the paper shape on the shelf;

- pointing to all the objects in the room that look like circles;

- beginning to identify and label shapes in their environment;

- making symmetrical designs with shape blocks.

Preschool-4

1 Begins to recognize and describe the attributes of shapes.

Four year olds begin to notice similarities and differences in the attributes of different shapes if attention is drawn to shapes in the classroom and environment. With encouragement, four year olds can recognize different variations of shapes (for example, equilateral triangles and isosceles triangles are all triangles), identify particular shapes in different orientations as being the same shape, and label shapes and discuss their characteristics. Demonstrating familiarity with geometric shapes includes:

- pointing out a triangle and counting its sides;

- labeling shapes by their feel rather than visually (for example, identifying shape blocks in a "feely box");

- locating individual shapes in pictures composed of overlapping shapes;

- announcing that a shape on a poster looks like "a triangle with its head cut off";

- matching and sorting shapes;

- recognizing an isosceles triangle as a triangle even when it is shown without a horizontal base;

- finding all the triangles that are exactly the same size.

Kindergarten

1 Recognizes and describes some attributes of shapes.

As children play with unit blocks, table blocks, pattern blocks, shape sorters, peg boards, and geoboards, they gain a concrete understanding of shape and form. Five year olds can identify, describe, label, and create a variety of common 2-D shapes and solids (circle, square, triangle, rectangle, cube, sphere) and begin to describe their attributes (corners, curves, edges). This concrete experience is important to later geometrical thinking and problem solving. Examples include:

- creating (drawing, folding, cutting) models of circles, squares, rectangles, and triangles with varied materials (for example, crayons, a geoboard, folding paper);

- describing characteristics of shapes (for example, a triangle has three straight sides);

- understanding that two triangles, even if they are oriented differently in space, are still triangles;

- recognizing that equilateral triangles, triangles with sides of different lengths, triangles with oblique angles, and triangles with right angles are all triangles.

First Grade

1 Recognizes attributes of shapes and relationships among shapes.

First graders can recognize, name, build, draw, and describe the defining attributes of 2-D shapes, including triangles, rectangles, squares, and circles. They can identify relationships between shapes (for example, "There are two red trapezoids inside the yellow hexagon."). Many children this age begin to explore 3-D shapes. By constructing and manipulating shapes, they develop spatial thinking. Examples of how first graders demonstrate this understanding include:

- comparing, matching, and reproducing shapes (for example, with tangrams, geoboards, pattern blocks);
- recognizing the relationships between shapes (for example, combining two triangles to create a square, or two trapezoids to form a hexagon);
- describing the defining attributes of shapes (for example, triangles have three corners, three sides);
- recognizing and comparing specific attributes of forms and shapes (number of sides, corners, faces).

Second Grade

1 Recognizes attributes of shapes and relationships among shapes.

Second graders can recognize and describe the attributes (size, color, etc.) and defining properties (what makes a square a square) of 2- and 3-D shapes (including triangles, squares, pentagons, hexagons, cubes, spheres, and cylinders). Using manipulative materials, they can construct shapes, create congruent shapes, and explore what happens when shapes are changed (adding or subtracting shapes to make new shapes). Examples include:

- comparing and describing attributes of shapes ("All triangles have three sides. Some are tall and thin; others, short and fat.");
- recognizing parts of shapes and how shapes are constructed ("This rectangle has a pair of short lines, two long lines, and four angles.");
- recognizing congruence even when shapes are presented from different perspectives;
- using shapes and their names in everyday experience (observing them in nature, using them to sort and classify objects);
- analyzing how shapes are made (for example, a hexagon has six sides, six corners, and three sets of parallel lines).

Third Grade

1 Analyzes properties and relationships among 2-D and 3-D shapes.

Third graders can recognize and describe the properties of plane and solid figures including parallelograms, hexagons, cubes, cones, and pyramids and classify them according to their properties using accurate mathematical language (correct names of shapes, words such as "angles," "sides," "faces," etc.). Using drawings, manipulatives, and computers, they explore the relationships among shapes by adding to them, dividing them, identifying shapes within other shapes, and creating congruent shapes. Examples include:

- drawing isosceles and equilateral triangles within a polygon;
- describing parts of shapes and how they are constructed (for example, rectangles have two pairs of equal length sides and four right angles);
- identifying points, lines, line segments, and angles;
- using toothpicks to create and label pentagons, hexagons, and octagons;
- using shapes and their names in everyday experience (observing them in nature, using them to sort and classify objects, creating designs that incorporate shapes).

III Mathematical Thinking

95

Preschool-3

2 Shows understanding of several positional words.

Three year olds tend to describe things in relation to their own position in space, but show understanding of common positional words when asked to place objects on top of or below something, or when asked to point to the bottom, or to indicate up and down. They can understand such positional words as "over," "under," "above," "on," and "next to." They show awareness of position by:

- putting their hands over their heads in response to a recorded movement song;
- finding the scotch tape when told it is on the art shelf next to the paper;
- noticing that they are standing in front of a classmate in a line or beside a classmate in the circle;
- correctly using positional words as they work, play, and perform routine tasks;
- placing their leg braces next to their mats at rest time when the teacher asks them to do so;
- commenting that the farm animal is on or in the box.

Preschool-4

2 Shows understanding of and uses several positional words.

Four year olds continue to develop spatial sense, which is the awareness of themselves in relation to the people and objects around them. They acquire the vocabulary of position and begin to learn about direction, distance, and location. By age four, children should understand a number of positional and directional words, such as "above," "below," "under," "beside," and "behind." They demonstrate this understanding by:

- knowing where to stand if asked to stand behind a classmate in the line;
- putting the bedroom dollhouse furniture in the same arrangement as the furniture in their apartments;
- using distance words like "near" and "far";
- verbalizing their positions as they work and play;
- going over to sit beside (or in front of) a classmate when asked to do so;
- placing felt cutouts of trees, a sandbox, swing, and slide to make a map of the playground;
- putting the ball under the chair when asked to do so.

Kindergarten

2 Shows understanding of and uses direction, location, and position words.

Children learn positional vocabulary as they develop spatial awareness and a recognition of symmetry and balance. Through discovery, experimentation, and experience, children form beginning understandings of direction (Which way?), distance (How far?), and location (Where?). Examples include:

- placing an object inside and outside, behind and in front, under and above, beside and on a box, and describing its changing locations;
- commenting that an object is nearer to me and farther from you;
- identifying who is sitting beside the teacher and who is sitting in front of her;
- completing an obstacle course that asks the runner to crawl through the tunnel, run behind the swings, run in front of the slide, jump beside the sandbox, and jump on the ramp;
- giving directions to a partner in the block area to place the curved block on top of the long rectangle block;
- using direction, location, and position words spontaneously as they participate in play activities.

First Grade

2 Explores and solves spatial problems using manipulatives and drawings.

First graders reveal their developing sense of order, design, and spatial organization as they create drawings, build with blocks and Legos, and use math manipulatives (such as pattern blocks, tangrams, and geoboards). Hands-on experiences that allow them to move in physical space and arrange and describe objects in space help them learn about location (Where?), distance (How far?), direction (Which way?), and positional vocabulary ("near," "far," "below," "above," "behind," "to the right" or "left of"). Examples include:

- giving or following directions for moving in space;
- giving directions for finding some needed materials using positional words (for example, "I think the pattern blocks are on the shelf below the scales, and maybe on the left side.");
- creating symmetrical designs using squares and triangles;
- visualizing slides, flips, and turns with 2-D shapes when using manipulatives or using a computer program;
- using simple coordinates to locate objects or pictures (for example, on a simple grid map of the neighborhood).

Second Grade

2 Explores and solves spatial problems using manipulatives and drawings.

Second graders develop spatial organization by working with objects to create shapes and designs, arranging and describing the object's location (Where?), distance (How far?), and direction (Which way?). They can explore and predict what will happen as they change the position of shapes in space (turns, flips, slides). Examples include:

- visualizing various solutions to spatial problems (for example, using pattern blocks to put five diamonds or 10 triangles into the outline of a flower);
- using simple coordinates to locate positions on a graph or map;
- creating a pattern block design and then copying the design onto grid paper;
- making a symmetrical design on a geoboard using only eight nails;
- experimenting with flips, turns, and slides (for example, analyzing how a design changes when rotated to a different position in space or completing a puzzle on a computer program).

Third Grade

2 Explores and solves spatial problems using manipulatives and drawings.

As third graders work with math manipulatives, drawings, and computers, they experiment with form and design, symmetry, reflections, and rotation. They can describe location (including finding points on a grid) and movement (flips, slides, and turns). Examples of the spatial problems they might solve include:

- visualizing various solutions to spatial problems (for example, using tangrams to create animals);
- making a symmetrical design using only 16 pattern blocks;
- predicting the results of flipping or turning 2-D shapes;
- composing and decomposing shapes (for example, creating a trapezoid from triangles and a square or locating many smaller shapes within a larger one);
- using coordinates to locate points on a grid;
- creating reflection drawings (using the same 10 pattern blocks to construct the other side of a 10-piece design).

Preschool-3

1 Shows understanding of some comparative words.

Words describing size are used frequently in everyday conversation (for example, "big," "little," "tall," "short," "long"). Three year olds are beginning to experiment with measurement concepts when they describe people and objects by:

- observing that the shell on the science table is very big;

- standing next to a classmate and observing that he is "taller than me";

- making a line of blocks and commenting that this road is "the longest one in the world";

- using measurement words when describing things to peers or the teacher (for example, talking about how long the bead necklace is, or announcing, "My block building is the biggest.").

Preschool-4

1 Orders, compares, and describes objects according to a single attribute.

Grouping things based on a single attribute that changes systematically (small to large, short to long, soft to loud) is called seriation. Ordering or seriation requires children to observe and distinguish slight differences among two or three objects. Four year olds begin to compare and seriate according to size, length, height, and weight as they explore the properties of things and decide which things are bigger, longer, shorter, or heavier. Demonstration of seriation and comparison skills includes:

- placing three crayons on the table, from the shortest to the longest, or the fattest to the thinnest;

- taking leaves brought in from a class walk and arranging them from biggest to smallest;

- noticing which children in the class are taller and which are shorter;

- "measuring" with a friend to find out who has the longer string of beads;

- figuring out with a classmate who has the bigger cookie;

- arranging four children in a line from shortest to tallest;

- using measurement words during the school day.

Kindergarten

1 Orders, compares, and describes objects by size, length, capacity, and weight.

Five year olds are very interested in ordering and comparing objects (for example, "You have more ice cream than I do."). They start by being able to order only four or five objects, and gradually increase to eight or ten. Many children begin to differentiate among size, length, and weight and use appropriate terms to describe each attribute. These direct comparisons of length, volume, and weight form the foundation for more complex measuring activities. Examples include:

- arranging six or seven rods from shortest to longest, left to right, top to bottom, or bottom to top;

- identifying the first, second, and third shape in a necklace, regardless of the orientation of the necklace (that is, left to right, right to left, top to bottom, bottom to top);

- making a display of several stones, arranged from smallest to largest;

- using a string or paper strip to compare the length of two objects;

- commenting that the outside door is heavier than the classroom door.

First Grade

1 Compares and describes objects by length, capacity, and weight.

As first graders measure and describe objects, they can name, discuss, and compare objects according to their attributes. In addition to using comparative words, they begin to use measurement terminology, such as "inches," "feet," "centimeters," and "meters." Examples include:

- identifying the heavier of two objects after weighing them on a balance scale;
- discussing the length and width of an object just measured, using terminology correctly;
- solving an area/array problem in which they know that there are three rows of three, by first setting out cubes, then counting "Three in this row, and three makes six," and then counting by ones, "seven, eight, and nine";
- noticing that only a ¼ cup of water is needed for the applesauce, so some water in the cup should be spilled out;
- comparing objects according to size (for example, "My hair is longer than yours." "This one weighs more.");
- comparing the height of two children and explaining that one is taller by a few inches.

Second Grade

1 Compares and describes objects by attributes that can be measured.

Second graders can name, discuss, distinguish, compare, and order objects according to attributes of length, volume, weight, area, and time. Exploration of measurement with non-standard and standard units enables second graders to understand that the measuring process consists of counting consistent measurement units. Some examples include:

- comparing lengths, heights, and weights using standard measures;
- finding the perimeter of the classroom using a yardstick or trundle wheel;
- finding the area of an array by multiplying the number in one row by the number of columns (for example, counting 4 in each row, 5 columns, 4, 8, 12, 16, 20 altogether);
- using measurement reference frames appropriately, such as explaining that the string needed is about a foot long;
- comparing weights of objects using balance scales.

Third Grade

1 Demonstrates understanding of attributes that can be measured.

By third grade, students recognize the importance of consistent units of measure and understand the attributes of objects and events that can be measured (such as length, width, height, volume, time, and temperature). They also acquire measurement reference frames (such as "about one foot" and "nearly one kilogram"). Examples include:

- carrying out simple conversions (for example, from hours to minutes);
- explaining why an estimate of a pumpkin's weight is logical;
- explaining how to find the area of a rectangle using an array and pointing out that you multiply one row by the number of columns and rows;
- using the correct vocabulary to describe measurements (square units for area, degrees for temperature, etc.);
- knowing whether an accurate or an estimated measurement is needed;
- using correct units when discussing measurement of time (seconds, minutes, hours, days).

III Mathematical Thinking

Preschool-3

2 Participates in measuring activities.

Three year olds enjoy using cups and measuring spoons in the dramatic play corner and are just beginning to understand the teacher's use of measuring cups for a cooking project. Children this age show awareness of measuring activities by:

- making sure that only one pinch of food goes into the fish tank;
- filling the big bottle in the water table with many small cups of water;
- pretending to measure the length of a road of blocks with a tape measure;
- finding the cup, and with the teacher's help, measuring one cup of flour for the play dough recipe;
- playing with a balance scale, pretending to weigh their dolls on a human scale, or using measuring cups and spoons at the sand table.

Preschool-4

2 Participates in measuring activities.

As four year olds learn about their world, they begin to explore length, height, and weight, although understanding weight is still difficult for them. They have limited awareness of time, although many four year olds recognize how events are sequenced (first we eat snack, then we have free time, then we go to the gym). Four year olds are curious and interested in the measuring tools that adults use and are eager to explore with them. Examples of measuring skills include:

- measuring the table with unit blocks, and noting that it is four blocks long;
- noting that they can fill the large bowl in the sand table with three small cups of sand;
- trying to balance the scale by putting various objects on each side;
- holding their hands about a foot apart to show how long their play dough snakes are;
- using measuring cups and spoons during a classroom cooking activity;
- using measuring tools at the workbench or water table;
- measuring the length of a block road or the height of a block tower.

Kindergarten

2 Explores common instruments for measuring during work or play.

Children are interested in the tools and instruments used by adults, although they are just beginning to explore conventional measurement tools. Their interest in trying measurement tools to see how they work is demonstrated by:

- using a balance scale when comparing the weights of objects;
- incorporating measuring tools into their dramatic play (for example, "We need a cup of flour for these pancakes.");
- asking for a yardstick so they can see if their block building is taller than the yardstick;
- using a ruler to measure the height of a plant;
- using measuring cups at the water table to measure water or tablespoons and teaspoons at the cooking table to add ingredients to the cookie recipe;
- using classroom measurement tools (scales, rulers, cups) for activities such as cooking, building, and describing items at the science center.

First Grade

See the following indicator
on page 97 in Mathematical
Thinking:

   D Geometry and spatial rela-
       tions

   2 Explores and solves spatial
       problems using manipula-
       tives and drawings.

Second Grade

See the following indicator
on page 97 in Mathematical
Thinking:

   D Geometry and spatial rela-
       tions

   2 Explores and solves spatial
       problems using manipula-
       tives and drawings.

Third Grade

See the following indicator
on page 97 in Mathematical
Thinking:

   D Geometry and spatial rela-
       tions

   2 Explores and solves spatial
       problems using manipula-
       tives and drawings.

III Mathematical Thinking

Preschool-3

See the following indicator on page 100 in Mathematical Thinking:

- E   Measurement
- 2   Participates in measuring activities.

Preschool-4

See the following indicator on page 100 in Mathematical Thinking:

- E   Measurement
- 2   Participates in measuring activities.

Kindergarten

3   Estimates and measures using non-standard and standard units.

When children begin to measure objects, they first select a unit of measurement, compare that unit to the object, and count the number of units required to represent the object. Five year olds spontaneously use such units as a foot, hand span, paper clip, or block to measure objects. They explore estimation with length, size, and volume. Examples include:

- guessing whether or not a container is big enough to hold all their marbles;
- measuring the length of a table by connecting cubes;
- estimating that a bird's nest weighs the same as five counting bears;
- stating that the road they just built is seven unit blocks long;
- using a common measuring stick to compare how long or tall things are.

First Grade

2 Uses simple tools and techniques to measure with non-standard and standard units.

By exploring measurement with non-standard and standard units, first graders acquire an understanding of the measuring process and the reasons for using consistent measuring units. They can estimate measurements and solve problems using different non-standard units and standard measures. They begin to learn the names, purposes, and methods of using tools such as balance scales, thermometers, and rulers. Some examples include:

- estimating length, height, or weight using non-standard measures (for example, hands, body lengths, blocks) and then checking predictions;

- using non-standard units to determine length, weight, and volume (unifix cubes, one-inch cubes, Cuisenaire rods);

- getting a ruler to measure the length of a table after estimating its length in inches;

- recognizing the uses of such standard measuring tools as rulers, scales, and thermometers, and the language that matches the tools (pounds and ounces for weight, inches and feet for length, degrees for thermometers).

Second Grade

2 Uses simple tools and techniques to estimate and measure.

Second graders can estimate measurements and check predictions while solving problems. They know the purpose of common measurement instruments (such as balance scales, thermometers, and rulers). With support from adults, they can begin to read the calibrated scales of standard measuring tools. Examples of children's skills include:

- using a balance scale to determine which of two objects is heavier or lighter;

- recognizing the uses of such standard measuring tools as rulers, scales, and thermometers, as well as the language that matches the tools (for example, ounces or kilograms for weight);

- measuring objects to determine weight and volume;

- measuring the length of the blackboard with several different non-standard measures and then explaining the reasons for a standard unit of measure;

- beginning to link measurements to what they refer to (four hamburgers weigh about a pound, a desk is about a meter high).

Third Grade

2 Uses tools and techniques to estimate and measure.

Third graders can estimate and solve measurement problems using standard instruments. They can be expected to read calibrated scales and begin to recognize that measurements often fall between whole numbers. Examples include:

- determining how much heavier, taller, or bigger one object is than another (for example, "The red magnet is five ounces heavier than the green one.");

- estimating the classroom perimeter and then measuring it with a trundle wheel;

- using reasonable estimates when measuring ("The bulletin board is about two yards long." "The pumpkin weighs about 2 ½ kilograms.");

- locating objects in the classroom that are a given length (5", 18 cm, etc.), then comparing results with classmates;

- estimating standard measures using reference frames (about one meter, about two pounds) and then checking predictions;

- measuring the length of an object and finding out it is 6⅜ inches long.

Preschool-3

Not expected at this level.

Preschool-4

Not expected at this level.

Kindergarten

4 **Shows awareness of time concepts.**

Initially, five year olds view time as a sequence of events of varied durations (eating breakfast comes before the bus ride to school and takes less time). Through experiences with classroom routines, schedules, clocks, and calendars, they begin to use words representing time ("morning," "afternoon," "evening," "day," "night," "yesterday," "tomorrow," "week," "month"), name the days of the week, and refer to time in more conceptual terms by:

- talking about the trip taken when "I went to school the day before this one";
- commenting that planting the seeds took all of free-choice time;
- knowing that the bus driver will come to pick them up after they play outside;
- labeling times of the day as morning or night time;
- knowing that it is winter because there is snow outside;
- asking a question about clocks or what time it is;
- telling a friend, "April is when my birthday comes and I will be six years old."

First Grade

3 Shows some understanding of time concepts.

First graders are developing an understanding of the sequence of events and the passage of time. They can sequence the days of the week and the months of the year. They can tell time using digital and analog clocks to the nearest hour and half hour. Examples of this understanding include:

- being able to name the days the class goes to gym;
- reading and using information on a calendar with some accuracy;
- recognizing repeating patterns of time (days, weeks, and months);
- making reasonable estimates of amounts of time (it takes one second to throw a ball, one hour to bake a cake, one month to grow a bean plant);
- ordering their day ("I wake up at 6 a.m. I go to school at 7 a.m. I go to sleep at 8 p.m.");
- looking at the clock and recognizing that in a few minutes it will be 11:30, which is time for lunch.

Second Grade

3 Shows some understanding of time concepts.

Second graders can read and use calendar information meaningfully. They can recognize familiar durations of time and tell and write time to the hour, half hour, and quarter hour. Some ways they demonstrate their understanding of time include:

- reading the calendar and stating, "November 7th, a Tuesday, is my brother's birthday.";
- recognizing repeating patterns of time (days, weeks, months, years, and seasons);
- making reasonable estimates about amounts of time (it would take 10 minutes to run a mile, a half hour to ride the bus to school, or about one month to grow a bean plant);
- ordering their day ("I wake up at 6:30 a.m. I go to school at 7:30 a.m. I go to sleep at 8:30 p.m.");
- observing that it is almost 3:30, and that's when the buses come.

Third Grade

3 Shows understanding of time concepts.

Third graders can recognize and use methods to keep track of time with calendars or clocks. They can tell time accurately using both analog and digital clocks. Examples of their understanding of time include:

- recognizing repeating patterns of time (days, weeks, months, years, and seasons);
- making predictions using calendars about when events will occur;
- estimating durations of time and checking estimates using a stop watch;
- ordering her/his day, week, or year ("In the fall I start school." "My science project is due in two weeks.");
- using a.m. and p.m. when discussing time;
- telling time on digital and analog clocks.

III Mathematical Thinking

⫿⫿⫿ Mathematical Thinking
F Data collection and probability

Preschool-3

Not expected at this level.

Preschool-4

Not expected at this level.

Kindergarten

1 Begins to collect data and make records using lists or graphs.

Collecting data, graphing, and interpreting graphs provide meaningful opportunities to count and make comparisons. Initially, five year olds are more interested in specific instances of data and lists ("Terry lives in a house and I live in an apartment.") than in classifying data into categories (10 children live in apartments, 8 live in houses, and 4 live in mobile homes). With teacher guidance, they can pose questions, collect data, and organize their observations using concrete objects, pictures, graphs, and lists. Examples include:

- setting up a chart in the block area to record who chooses to use blocks each day;

- looking at the graph that shows different ways children get to school and counting to find out that seven children take the bus and six are walkers;

- listing the foods given to the hamster regularly, then discussing how often the hamster ate each type of food;

- predicting that seven children will buy lunch tomorrow, after looking at the graph showing which children who brought or bought lunch last week.

First Grade

1 Collects, records, and interprets data using simple tallies, lists, charts, and graphs.

First graders recognize that data can be organized according to categories and displayed in different ways. Content across the curriculum provides children with meaningful experiences to learn how to organize and represent data. As they conduct simple surveys and create real or concrete graphs, first graders develop the skills of reading, interpreting, and comparing information. Examples include:

- designing a simple class survey, creating categories, and then representing the data graphically (for example, about favorite foods, number of brothers and sisters);

- tallying collected data (on questions such as, "How many children want apples or bananas for snack?");

- creating a concrete graph of "How we get to school" using green unifix cubes for buses, red ones for cars, and yellow ones for walking, or a simple picture graph (pictures of buses, cars, and feet);

- saying how many children have birthdays in each month after reading a graph to figure out which month has the most birthdays.

Second Grade

1 Collects, records, and interprets data using tallies, lists, charts, and graphs.

Seven year olds formulate questions, collect data to answer them, organize information, and evaluate the effectiveness of graphical representations. They can organize and display data through simple numerical summaries such as counts, tables, and tallies, as well as graphical displays such as tables, bar graphs, and line graphs. Making graphs part of science and social studies activities helps children view graphing as an efficient way to organize information and teaches them to read and interpret organized data. Examples include:

- conducting a class survey to collect data and then creating a bar graph as a representation;

- tallying collected data (on questions such as how many children want to play kickball, tether ball, or jump rope at recess);

- using a graphics program on a computer to create different types of graphs (picture, bar, pie, and line) and discussing the features of each and their advantages;

- keeping track of time spent on homework each night and creating a bar graph from the data.

Third Grade

1 Collects, records, and interprets data using tallies, lists, charts, and graphs.

Eight year olds can organize information numerically and in categories in many different ways, including lists, charts, tallies, and graphs. They can identify different parts of a graph (title, labels, and key) and can generate and respond to questions about information presented in an organized way. Examples include:

- conducting a class survey and collecting data (for example, about favorite sports);

- identifying the range, median, and mode for baseball scores for the season and discussing how these numbers are used in baseball;

- observing and graphing temperature changes over time using a computer;

- generating problems that involve collecting and organizing information and then representing the information on a chart or graph (dividing photographs of animals into multiple groups based on features of their habitats);

- interpreting and comparing information presented on a bar graph in a newspaper.

III Mathematical Thinking

III Mathematical Thinking

F   Data collection and probability

Preschool-3

Not expected at this level.

Preschool-4

Not expected at this level.

Kindergarten

See the following indicator on page 106 in Mathematical Thinking:

F Data collection and probability

1 Begins to collect data and make records using lists or graphs.

First Grade

2 Begins to make predictions based on data.

With encouragement, first graders can begin to reflect on information and evaluate the likelihood of events or situations. As they make predictions and listen to those of others, they can discuss whether their predictions are reasonable. Examples include:

- offering an explanation about the likelihood of it snowing and saying, "We live where it is always warm and it never snows";
- sorting two packages of M&Ms and predicting how many reds there will be in a third package;
- recording the outdoor temperature for several days and then making a prediction about the next day's temperature;
- rolling two dice 20 times, keeping track of the sums, and then predicting the next five rolls;
- charting how many people in the class prefer apples or bananas and then predicting whether the other first grade classes will have the same results.

Second Grade

2 Begins to make predictions based on data.

Second graders can reflect on information they collect and think about whether some events are more likely to happen than others. As they keep track of different kinds of events (rolling dice, flipping coins, or the weather), they begin to learn that some things can be predicted and others can not. Examples include:

- noticing patterns on a graph and making a prediction based on the patterns;
- predicting coin tosses after reviewing charted information;
- predicting which of two events is more likely to occur after experimenting (for example, using a spinner);
- beginning to use language such as "likely," "equally likely," "least likely" when making a prediction.

Third Grade

2 Makes predictions based on data.

When third graders have repeated opportunities to analyze information, they begin to understand that "chance" refers to the likelihood of an event occurring. They can use the terminology of probability ("likely," "certain," "uncertain") to describe their predictions. Some ways students demonstrate this skill include:

- creating a chart to show all the possible outcomes of a probability situation;
- noticing patterns on a weather graph;
- predicting what might happen next after studying a graph that shows the results of successive coin tosses;
- predicting the winning soccer team based on repeated observations of games during the season and using words like "most likely," "least likely," "equally likely."

III Mathematical Thinking

Scientific Thinking

This domain addresses central areas of scientific investigation: inquiry skills, physical, life, and earth sciences. The processes of scientific investigation are emphasized throughout because process skills are embedded in—and fundamental to—all science instruction and content. The domain's focus is on how children actively investigate through observing, recording, describing, questioning, forming explanations, and drawing conclusions.

Preschool-3

1 Uses senses to observe and explore classroom materials and natural phenomena.

Three year olds are very curious. They naturally explore and study most common objects and living things. They will study an ant crawling on the sidewalk or an interesting twig they find lying on the ground. They are more apt to express their wonder about the world by commenting about their observations than by asking meaningful questions. Examples include:

- looking at pine cones and pointing out every detail they see or feel (such as the points and the sticky stuff);

- listening to the call of a bird and asking a friend or teacher to listen as well;

- noticing a bulb stalk grow taller each day, and wondering what the "fat ball" on top will become;

- trying to guess the identity of objects from their smell;

- observing the gerbil and saying how funny his mouth looks when he eats;

- wondering where bubbles come from when water is shaken in a plastic jar or tube;

- listening to an audio tape of sounds and guessing what the sounds are (for example, running water or an airplane).

Preschool-4

1 Asks questions and uses senses to observe and explore materials and natural phenomena.

Exploration is the heart of the four year old's world. Looking, touching, lifting, listening, and experimenting are all very natural at this age. They are just beginning to articulate their observations about the world in an organized way. In the course of play, children's experiences lead them to raise such questions as, "What will happen if…?" With teacher guidance, children can be led to answer questions through further observation, making charts, or otherwise organizing observations into information that helps them understand their explorations. Examples include:

- exploring at the water or sand table, letting the sand or water run through their fingers, commenting on the way it feels, and noting how fast or slow it flows;

- observing ice cubes or snow at room temperature to see what happens;

- listening to sounds from outside and identifying the sources (for example, "That's a truck, that's an airplane, that's a dog barking.");

- taking apart a flashlight to see what is inside;

- wondering where frost comes from that appears on windows after cold nights.

Kindergarten

1 Seeks information through observation, exploration, and descriptive investigations.

Five year olds' natural curiosity about their world frequently leads them to ask, "Why?" As questions are raised, kindergartners seek answers primarily through exploration, manipulation, and careful observation using their senses. After observing, children need adult help to organize their observations into thoughts that will assist them in making further discoveries. They enjoy the challenge of sorting objects, making comparisons, seeing patterns in nature, and noticing differences and similarities. Examples include:

- becoming more accurate and precise when reporting observations (for example, counting the number of ridges on a shell or trying to use all senses when observing);

- inspecting a bird's nest carefully and commenting about how it was constructed;

- working with wheeled vehicles, slopes, and differently-shaped objects to find out how they move;

- figuring out ways, with teacher help, to investigate phenomena they have observed, such as plants growing, the effect of pollution, or change in the seasons.

First Grade

1 Seeks information through active investigation.

For first graders, investigation includes observing, collecting, counting, measuring, and comparing things, and then attempting to organize this information in order to interpret it. Children this age naturally have questions. They can obtain answers to their questions through careful observation, by setting up simple tests, and by applying previously learned scientific knowledge to new situations. Modeling by the teacher encourages first graders to ask scientific questions that extend "Why?" to "What?" and "How?" ("How can we find out?" "What will happen if...?") Examples of how first graders engage in scientific investigations include:

- setting out different food samples and observing which foods the hamster seems to prefer;
- collecting different types of pine cones in order to have a large sample to sort and classify;
- looking at pictures and captions in books and magazines to find information related to a particular question.

Second Grade

1 Seeks information through active investigation.

The process of investigation includes collecting, observing, counting, comparing, and measuring things, and organizing information in ways that make interpretation easier. Second graders can observe carefully, take time to notice details, and with some prompting, ask scientific questions such as, "How can we find out...?" "What will happen if...?" They can pose questions and answer them through various techniques such as setting up simple tests or applying previously learned scientific knowledge to new situations. Examples include:

- using focused observation to answer specific questions (watching the frog to see how it catches and eats crickets);
- using books, magazines, and charts to help answer questions;
- setting up experiments to test ideas (leaving bowls with the same amount of water in different parts of the classroom and monitoring how long it takes for the water in each bowl to evaporate).

Third Grade

1 Seeks information through active investigation.

The process of scientific inquiry involves posing questions that can be answered through careful observation and investigation and then comparing findings with existing scientific knowledge. Third graders can pose questions and then answer them using various techniques, including observing over time, collecting data, setting up a simple controlled experiment, and applying previously learned scientific knowledge to new situations. Examples are:

- planning and conducting an experiment, including control of one variable, with some guidance from a teacher (testing to see how fast the ball rolls when the angle of the ramp or size of the ball changes);
- using books, magazines, charts, and computer databases to find information that supports a hypothesis about a student-generated question;
- after sorting and classifying materials, asking a "What would happen if...?" question and then thinking through how to set up an experiment to find out.

IV Scientific Thinking

Preschool-3

2 Begins to use simple tools and equipment for investigation.

Three year olds do not have much experience focusing on specific characteristics of objects. Tools (magnifiers, lenses, and eye droppers) can help them attend to a particular object or specific aspects of an object. Children need time to manipulate tools before they are taught how to use them. Examples of children using tools for investigation include:

- looking at a variety of objects through a large magnifying glass embedded in a tripod;
- using an egg beater to whip up bubbles in the water table;
- looking at various objects through a hand lens;
- using an eye dropper to drop food coloring into water;
- pumping water out of a liquid soap container or a baster;
- repeatedly making a water wheel spin around at the water table.

Preschool-4

2 Uses simple tools and equipment for investigation.

Four year olds are just beginning to plan their investigations. They enjoy using tools that help them focus on an object and define the characteristics they are trying to describe. Children show interest in using tools for scientific investigation by:

- trying to sift a variety of materials through a sieve to see what will go through and what will not;
- using a hand lens to look at ridges on an earthworm;
- using an eye dropper to drop color in glasses of water;
- getting a better look at a bird at the birdfeeder with binoculars;
- observing objects through a hand lens and then through a simple microscope;
- using a wire whisk to whip up bubbles in a bowl.

Kindergarten

2 Uses simple tools and equipment to extend the senses and gather data.

Although kindergartners begin to observe using their five senses, they are very intrigued with tools that extend the power of their senses and that they associate with grown-up activities. Scientific tools include magnifiers, gears and pulleys, calculators and computers, and simple balance scales and rulers. With regular use of a variety of tools, young children begin to recognize how technology helps us perform tasks more easily. Ways that children show their interest in scientific tools include:

- placing two rocks on the balance scale to find out which one is heavier;
- looking at all kinds of things through a hand lens;
- examining a bicycle chain and gear sprockets and trying to figure out how these make the wheels turn;
- outlining shadows of objects with chalk and measuring them at different times of the day;
- checking indoor and outdoor temperatures with a thermometer;
- experimenting with tubes and funnels at the sand and water tables.

First Grade

2 Recognizes some ways tools and technology are used to gather scientific information.

First graders can begin to use tools to help them gather scientific data. As they use containers, scales, rulers, thermometers, clocks, magnifiers, or computers, they can think about how each tool is used as well as how it improves their scientific investigations. Examples include:

- proposing the proper tools and devices to help with an observation (placing an insect in a jar, covering the jar with aluminum foil, and using a pencil to poke holes in the foil so the insect can breathe);
- using a balance to test an idea that the bigger something is, the more it weighs;
- using a magnifier to observe the veins in a leaf more closely and then drawing a picture of the leaf;
- using a CD-ROM to view pictures of insects from South America and comparing these insects to insects collected near the school;
- checking the outdoor thermometer before going out to recess to determine if they need to wear sweaters;
- using binoculars to look more closely at the colors of the birds outside the classroom.

Second Grade

2 Recognizes some ways tools and technology can be used to gather scientific information.

Second graders can gather scientific data using tools such as scales, rulers, thermometers, containers, glass slides, magnifiers, and computers. They can think about how each tool can be used, as well as why and how it helps with scientific investigation. Examples of how they use scientific tools include:

- using appropriate tools to measure length, volume, and weight;
- using a CD-ROM or the Internet to view pictures of desert animals in order to consider how physical characteristics of animals are affected by the environment in which they live;
- using a magnifier to observe the details of a caterpillar chrysalis;
- using scales and rulers to measure objects and then classify them according to their measurements;
- separating fabric fibers with tweezers to examine them more closely.

Third Grade

2 Demonstrates some understanding of how tools and technology advance scientific investigation.

Third graders select and use tools and technology to help them conduct effective scientific investigations. As they use materials, supplies, and equipment in safe and appropriate ways, their awareness of how scientists use and invent tools to solve scientific problems increases. Examples of their understanding of ways to use tools for scientific investigation include:

- using thermometers to measure temperature (air, sand, water, humans);
- explaining why it is necessary to wear safety goggles before experimenting with solutions;
- choosing the correct tools to measure the weight of different objects accurately;
- using a graphing software program to make a bar graph to record growth over time;
- gathering research data from the Internet;
- using a meter stick to determine the length of a variety of objects.

Preschool-3

3 Makes comparisons among objects.

Three year olds enjoy calling attention to details and exploring, with adult support, the ways in which things are alike or different. They comment on what they see, but need to be given words to describe more accurately what they are observing. Examples include:

- examining a shell collection and responding to requests such as, "Find some more pink ones" or " Show me a shell that isn't smooth";
- looking at pictures of bugs in a book and observing that some of them have wings and some of them do not;
- floating and sinking various objects in the water table;
- observing differences among the birds in the yard or at the feeder;
- telling whether the sounds made by rhythm instruments are the same or different.

Preschool-4

3 Makes comparisons among objects.

Four year olds readily make comparisons about observed objects when encouraged and guided. They become enthusiastic about different kinds of paw prints in the snow or differences in footprints in the sand. They enjoy finding things that are the same or different. Their "comparative statements" represent how very young children begin to draw conclusions from observations. Children show this by:

- comparing the properties of objects that float in water with objects that sink;
- describing and comparing a variety of fabrics at the collage table such as satin, corduroy, felt, and taffeta;
- noting the difference in speed when a truck is pushed over tiles or rugs;
- collecting a variety of leaves on a walk in the fall, looking at them carefully, and describing differences in shape, edges, color, or size;
- comparing their handprints to those of their classmates.

Kindergarten

3 Forms explanations and communicates scientific information.

Scientific thinking requires observing, asking questions, drawing conclusions, and proposing explanations about current and future events. Children can begin to guess the reasons for what they have observed—even if those reasons are not "scientifically correct"—as they organize, with teacher support and guidance, the information they have gathered. Five year olds communicate scientific information through speaking, drawing, and writing. Evidence of these growing skills includes:

- feeling a conch shell and explaining that it has all those bumps and prongs so that there will be more room inside;
- offering an explanation for why colors mixed together create new colors;
- measuring and recording on a class chart the height of a bean plant and explaining why other plants have different heights;
- describing the rule they used for sorting the shells into two different groups;
- guessing that a sponge will sink in the water because it is bigger than a plastic boat that floated.

First Grade

3 Forms explanations and communicates scientific information.

Using observation and information to construct reasonable explanations and presenting these explanations to others are critical skills for first graders. As first graders observe and conduct simple investigations, they can record their work with drawings and simple captions. With prompts from a teacher (such as, "What do you think will happen if...?"), they can make a prediction and collect data to confirm or disprove their prediction. They can describe their findings and propose simple explanations based on their data. Examples include:

- deciding which type of material bounces highest by dropping different kinds of balls from various heights and recording the findings;

- describing the best growing conditions for a plant, after systematically varying light, water, and growing media;

- offering an explanation based on prior knowledge when asked, "How do you know that's the reason?";

- drawing and writing about the movement of a hermit crab and then explaining why the crab moved in different directions.

Second Grade

3 Forms explanations and communicates scientific information.

Observations and data collection are critical ingredients in the construction of reasonable scientific explanations. As second graders observe and conduct experiments, they record what they see and do using drawings, written descriptions, charts, and graphs. They can describe their findings and begin to summarize the data. They can analyze their findings by asking and answering questions such as, "Why did you decide to do it that way?" and "Why do you think this happened?" Examples include:

- explaining that wheels and inclined planes make work easier, following several tests to find this out;

- describing the best growing conditions for a plant, after systematically varying light, water, and growing media;

- developing ideas about types of materials that will disintegrate quickly through burying different objects in soil for several weeks;

- using a bar graph to record and describe information gathered over time and then explaining why they thought that this kind of graph would best illustrate their findings.

Third Grade

3 Forms explanations and communicates scientific information in a variety of ways.

Third graders can use the evidence they collect from investigations and their prior knowledge to make predictions, draw inferences, and construct reasonable explanations. They can communicate their findings in different formats (including graphs, charts, and reports) using correct scientific terminology. Some ways a child shows evidence of this skill are:

- collecting evidence through investigation and then analyzing it to draw a logical conclusion;

- measuring and graphing outdoor temperatures using accurate terminology (degrees Celsius);

- recognizing a pattern on a graph showing at what time the moon was over his house each night and offering a logical explanation for it;

- analyzing a peer's explanation and questioning its reasonableness;

- collecting data over time, recording observations in a science journal, reviewing the data, and drawing a conclusion based on evidence.

IV Scientific Thinking

Preschool-3

See the following indicator on page 112 in Scientific Thinking:

A Inquiry

1 Uses senses to observe and explore classroom materials and natural phenomena.

Preschool-4

See the following indicator on page 112 in Scientific Thinking:

A Inquiry

1 Asks questions and uses senses to observe and explore materials and natural phenomena.

Kindergarten

1 Identifies, describes, and compares properties of objects.

Five year olds' continued sensory exploration enables them to understand the properties of objects in greater detail. With prompts from the teacher, they notice what things are made of and describe numerous attributes of objects including size, shape, color, texture, weight, temperature, whether objects are attracted or unaffected by magnets, and whether various objects sink or float. Although five year olds may watch with wonder as snow melts or water freezes, they have only a rudimentary understanding of the reasons for changes in state from solid to liquid to gas. Examples include:

- describing the differences between ice and water;
- taking apart a flashlight to see what is inside;
- exploring absorption as they try a variety of different materials (paper towel, a piece of cotton cloth, netting, wax paper) in shallow dishes of water to see which absorbs more water;
- creating ramps made of blocks and running various sizes of cars down the ramps to see if some cars go faster than others.

First Grade

1 Observes, describes, and compares properties, position, and motion of objects.

Six year olds can sort, classify, and describe objects in terms of their physical properties (including size, weight, shape, and color). Through active investigation, they can observe and describe how properties of objects change (for example, heating, cutting, freezing) and move (in different ways, at different speeds, and as a result of force). Some ways first graders demonstrate their growing understanding include:

- observing and describing how the texture of the clay changed after water was added;
- describing the position of objects in relation to fixed points (for example, the location of the art shelves relative to the windows);
- making logical (though often erroneous) predictions as a result of careful observations ("I don't think the Styrofoam ball will float because it is solid and all the other things we tested so far that were solid sank.");
- using tools such as a balance or magnifier to describe the physical properties of an object.

Second Grade

1 Identifies, describes, and compares properties, position, and motion of objects.

Second graders use physical properties (size, weight, shape, color, and temperature) to sort, classify, compare, and measure objects. They can identify the materials from which objects are made, describe how the properties of objects can be changed (by heating, cutting, freezing, etc.), and begin to understand that materials exist in different states (liquids, solids, and gases). Through active investigation, they explore position and motion (moving things in different ways and altering speed and force). Some ways they demonstrate their growing understanding include:

- observing carefully to see how physical properties may affect the action or motion of objects (seeing if the metal marble travels down the ramp faster or slower than the glass one);
- measuring the distances a toy car travels when pushed with different amounts of force;
- observing similarities and differences among groups of objects and naming groups based on the findings (for example, substances that are soluble and insoluble in water).

Third Grade

1 Identifies, describes, and compares properties, position, and motion of objects.

Third graders can observe, describe, measure, and classify the properties of objects including size, weight, shape, color, and temperature. They can describe matter as a liquid, solid, or gas and ways that matter can be changed (for example, by heating or freezing). They have learned that all matter is made of atoms which are too small to be seen with the naked eye. Through active investigation, they deepen their understanding of motion and forces. Some ways they demonstrate their growing understanding of these physical science concepts include:

- observing sophisticated properties of different types of matter (for example, buoyancy, transparency, melting points);
- classifying machines by specific properties (those using levers, pulleys, or inclined planes);
- combining substances to make new ones and comparing and measuring their properties or separating mixtures into their original substances;
- experimenting with evaporation of liquids under different conditions.

Ⅳ Scientific Thinking

B   Physical science

Preschool-3	Preschool-4	Kindergarten
Not expected at this level.	Not expected at this level.	See the following indicator on page 118 in Scientific Thinking:

Kindergarten

See the following indicator on page 118 in Scientific Thinking:

B Physical Science

1 Identifies, describes, and compares properties of objects.

First Grade

2 Explores and describes observable properties of light, heat, electricity, magnetism, and sound.

First graders are eager to investigate familiar phenomena such as light, heat, electricity, magnetism, and sound. As they conduct simple experiments (for example, holding flashlights in front of paper, figuring out which objects can be picked up by magnets), they learn how to respond to the question, "What happens when…?" Their attempts to explain these phenomena are based on their experience rather than on an abstract understanding of the concept of energy. Examples include:

- measuring and adding different amounts of water to a row of jars, striking the jars with a spoon, and observing the differences in sounds;
- experimenting with a flashlight to make shadows of different sizes and shapes;
- observing, measuring, and describing shadows;
- investigating a collection of objects, determining what the magnet will pick up and what it will not pick up, and sorting the objects accordingly;
- making a list of things in the home that use electricity and describing what happens when the electricity is turned off.

Second Grade

2 Explores and describes the observable properties of light, heat, electricity, magnetism, and sound.

Second graders can predict, experiment with, and describe the observable properties of light, heat, electricity, magnetism, and sound. Investigations of these phenomena lead them to understand that light travels in a straight line and can go through some materials but not others; heat is produced in many ways; electricity in circuits produces heat and light; and sound is caused by vibrations. Students' explanations are based on observation of action, rather than on the abstract concept of energy. Examples include:

- listening carefully to detect pitch differences created by stretching rubber bands to different lengths and then plucking them to make them vibrate;
- having experimented with bulbs, wires, and batteries before, predicting that the bulb will light up only if the wires are hooked up in a particular way;
- attempting to explain why shadows are longer or shorter at different times during the day, after repeated observations.

Third Grade

2 Demonstrates some understanding of the properties of light, heat, electricity, magnetism, and sound.

Third graders can identify different forms and sources of energy and, through experimentation, begin to consider how energy is changed from one form to another. They can describe some properties of light, heat, and sound. Their increasing ability to grasp abstract concepts leads third graders to begin to grapple with the concept of energy. Examples of their developing understanding of energy include:

- experimenting with flashlights to learn about the conditions under which light can be reflected, refracted, and absorbed;
- observing machines used in the home to see which ones convert energy into motion or heat;
- experimenting with circuits, batteries, and bulbs;
- predicting the size of shadows at different times of the day and then measuring and charting actual sizes;
- using a variety of materials to find out how sounds are changed by a change in vibrations.

IV Scientific Thinking

Preschool-3

See the following indicator on page 112 in Scientific Thinking:

A Inquiry

1 Uses senses to observe and explore classroom materials and natural phenomena.

Preschool-4

See the following indicator on page 112 in Scientific Thinking:

A Inquiry

1 Asks questions and uses senses to observe and explore materials and natural phenomena.

Kindergarten

1 **Observes and describes characteristics, basic needs, and life cycles of living things.**

By studying plants and animals, kindergarten children begin to differentiate living and non-living things. Five year olds can investigate the physical characteristics, basic needs, ways of moving, habitats, growth patterns, and life cycles of plants and animals common to their local area. They begin to learn about the relationships between animals and plants and the environments in which they live. Examples include:

• noting the different ways that insects move (for example, by crawling, hopping, and flying);

• smelling flowers and commenting on their odors;

• drawing a picture of a corn plant and labeling the roots, stem, and leaves;

• using the proper names for animal offspring (for example, "colt" rather than "baby horse") and matching animal offspring to their parents;

• classifying leaves collected on a nature walk according to their shape and color.

IV Scientific Thinking

First Grade

1 **Observes and describes characteristics, basic needs, and life cycles of living things.**

First graders can observe and describe the physical characteristics of living things and begin to generalize that all living things have basic needs. As they study plants and animals, children can explore the relationships among physical characteristics, basic needs, and the environments in which these live. First graders can grasp that all living things have a life cycle and begin to explore how life cycles differ from one living thing to another. Examples include:

- using non-standard measures to describe the differences in the lengths of various leaves;
- drawing detailed pictures showing specific characteristics of living things (for example, plants of different sizes, colors, and leaf shapes);
- planning, planting, and charting growth over time of their own gardens;
- drawing and labeling pictures of the class pet's eating habits;
- using a magnifier to observe the structure and materials of a bird's nest and offering an explanation for why these items were probably used;
- sorting a collection into two categories: living things and non-living things.

Second Grade

1 **Observes and describes characteristics, basic needs, and life cycles of living things.**

Second graders can observe and describe the physical characteristics and basic needs of organisms. As they study plants and animals, they can explore the relationship among physical characteristics, basic needs, and the environments in which organisms live. Second graders understand that living things have life cycles which include birth, growth, reproduction, and death, but that these cycles vary from one species to another. Examples include:

- observing and relating the parts of a plant to their function;
- describing how the guinea pig comes out of its hiding place to eat whenever it hears someone opening the cage door;
- explaining, after observing and recording the chick eggs hatching, "The chicks look a lot like the mother when they hatched, but much, much littler. But after they grow, they'll look the same as her.";
- showing an understanding of basic needs by explaining why the plants died during vacation ("We didn't water them for two weeks and someone accidentally turned off their special light.").

Third Grade

1 **Observes and describes characteristics and life cycles of living things.**

Third graders can describe the characteristics and basic needs of living organisms. They understand that while all living things have a life cycle that includes birth, growth, reproduction, and death, the life cycle varies from one species to another. As they explore the life cycles of different living things, they can begin to consider the concept of inherited traits. Examples include:

- responding thoughtfully to a teacher's question, such as, "How could you find out how a frog's eating habits change throughout its life cycle?";
- explaining how the earthworm moves after carefully observing one for several days;
- categorizing types of plants according to their adaptations to the environment;
- observing a variety of offspring and describing the similarities and differences between offspring and parent;
- comparing the life cycles of certain insects, frogs, chicks, and humans;
- gathering information from a web site about the life cycle of the bat and how bats care for their young.

IV Scientific Thinking
C   Life science

Preschool-3

Not expected at this level.

Preschool-4

Not expected at this level.

Kindergarten

See the following indicator on page 112 in Scientific Thinking:

A Inquiry

1 Seeks information through observation, exploration, and descriptive investigations.

First Grade

See the following indicator on page 113 in Scientific Thinking:

A Inquiry

1 Seeks information through active investigation.

Second Grade

See the following indicator on page 113 in Scientific Thinking:

A Inquiry

1 Seeks information through active investigation.

Third Grade

2 **Understands the relationship between the basic needs of organisms and their environment.**

Third graders understand that organisms can only survive in environments in which their basic needs can be met. By this age, students recognize that environments differ greatly and can consider the relationships among organisms' physical characteristics, basic needs, and the environments in which they live. Examples include:

• researching the food chain of organisms living in a river;

• creating a compost heap in a garden outside the school to investigate ways decomposition and decay support other living things;

• doing an Internet search to find information about birds living in different environments (for example, wetlands, deserts, forests) and then writing a research report;

• exploring plants and animals found in the desert by taking a "virtual desert tour" on the Internet;

• creating a chart showing behaviors of animals that enable them to survive in their environment (for example, migration, hibernation, growing a winter coat).

Preschool-3

See the following indicator on page 112 in Scientific Thinking:

A Inquiry

1 Uses senses to observe and explore classroom materials and natural phenomena.

Preschool-4

See the following indicator on page 112 in Scientific Thinking:

A Inquiry

1 Asks questions and uses senses to observe and explore materials and natural phenomena.

Kindergarten

1 **Explores and identifies properties of rocks, soil, water, and air.**

In kindergarten, children learn about the composition of the earth and the conservation of its resources. Five year olds can learn about the properties of rocks, soil, water, and air. They begin to identify how these materials are used and why it is important for people to use them carefully. Their growing knowledge and skills include:

• bringing in a collection of stones and looking at them through a magnifying glass, noting that some of them have lighter streaks and some of them have sparkles;

• checking the plants growing in sandy soil and noticing they are not growing as fast as the plants in other types of soil;

• looking at sand and dirt through a magnifying glass and describing how they are the same and different;

• exploring properties of air by blowing through a straw to spread paint on paper and noticing how the paint moves differently depending on how hard they blow;

• noting differences between wet and dry sand and how each is used in different ways when building sand structures.

First Grade

1 Explores and identifies properties and uses of rocks, soil, water, and air.

First graders are learning about the composition of the earth and the conservation of its resources. Through many active investigations, they develop the vocabulary to sort, classify, describe, and compare the properties of rocks, soil, water, and air. They can identify some ways people use (and abuse) these materials. Examples of their growing knowledge and skills include:

- sorting and classifying a collection of stones by their texture (for example, rough, smooth, bumpy);
- listing different objects made of rock;
- using a magnifier to examine a container of dry sand and describing the sand's properties;
- generating a list of ways to conserve water in the home;
- predicting how far different-sized balloons will fly when the air is let out of them and explaining why they made these predictions;
- observing and describing soil samples taken from different parts of the community and developing possible explanations for the differences.

Second Grade

1 Explores and identifies properties and uses of rocks, soil, water, and air.

As second graders continue to learn about the composition of the earth, they begin to understand that rocks and soil are solids, water is a liquid (or when frozen, a solid), and the air in our atmosphere is a gas. They understand that living things exist on or near the earth's surface, and they can identify some ways living things use (and abuse) the earth's resources. Examples include:

- observing and describing different soil samples using the properties of color and texture;
- making a list of different ways people use rocks, soil, air, and water;
- creating a bar graph of different kinds of rocks found on the playground;
- creating a water cycle in a plastic bag, then drawing a chart that illustrates the water cycle;
- explaining that the fossils seen at the museum tell us about life a long time ago;
- sorting, comparing, and describing samples of rocks, gravel, sand, and clay.

Third Grade

1 Demonstrates understanding of properties and uses of the earth's materials.

Third graders can identify the materials the earth is made of (rocks and soils, water, and the gases of the atmosphere). They begin to understand that these materials have different properties and that their properties affect their use as natural resources. They also recognize how misuse results in the destruction of natural resources. Some ways eight years olds demonstrate their understanding include:

- offering an explanation of the conditions that must be present for clouds to form after experimenting with freezing, condensation, precipitation, and evaporation;
- using computer software to create a chart showing the water cycle;
- observing, describing, and classifying soil samples and hypothesizing which types of plants might grow in each;
- using several different sources to gather information about fossils;
- experimenting with kites to observe the movement of wind;
- describing how methane gas from an incinerator causes air pollution.

Preschool-3

See the following indicator on page 112 in Scientific Thinking:

A Inquiry

1 Uses senses to observe and explore classroom materials and natural phenomena.

Preschool-4

See the following indicator on page 112 in Scientific Thinking:

A Inquiry

1 Asks questions and uses senses to observe and explore materials and natural phenomena.

Kindergarten

2 **Begins to observe and describe simple seasonal and weather changes.**

As young children learn to observe and experiment with scientific phenomena, they notice change and patterns. Studying the weather, sky, and seasons provides five year olds with concrete examples of nature's patterns and changes. In group activities, kindergarten children can identify, describe, and record daily changes in the weather, noticing wind speed, variations in the sky, air temperature, precipitation, and seasonal patterns of change. Examples include:

- naming the four seasons and realizing that they form a pattern because they repeat;

- noting that a grey sky means it might rain;

- commenting that at night the sun goes away and the moon appears;

- describing and recording the day's weather on a chart, noting temperature and other weather conditions;

- reminding a friend to put on boots for recess, because there is still snow on the playground;

- recognizing the pattern of lightning followed by thunder during a storm.

First Grade

2 Observes and describes simple changes in the earth and sky.

First graders can be encouraged to observe and describe patterns and changes in the earth and sky. As they observe and describe the weather and seasons, they can make predictions based on their observations. They can identify in basic terms the location, movement, and features of the sun, moon, and stars. Some examples of their growing understanding of the earth and sky include:

- observing and describing the differences between day and night;
- using a balance to determine the weights of various rocks;
- using a thermometer to determine the daily temperature and recording the temperature on a weather graph;
- telling the class about looking at constellations in the night sky using both the naked eye and binoculars;
- drawing pictures of the moon every day to keep track of the changes in its shape, then making a prediction about what shape it will be the next day;
- examining the weather chart and noticing that the temperature is getting warmer each day as "we get closer to summer vacation."

Second Grade

2 Observes and describes simple changes in the earth and sky.

Second graders can observe and describe patterns and changes in the earth and sky. As they observe and describe the weather and seasons, they can make predictions based on their observations. They can describe the location, movement, and features of the sun, moon, and stars. Examples include:

- recording and graphing changes in temperature and weather conditions over time;
- watching the weather channel or using weather information from the Internet to keep track of sunrise and sunset for a week, then explaining that the sun rises and sets in a pattern every 24 hours;
- working with a partner to draw and measure shadows;
- drawing a picture of the night sky and including the moon and a few constellations of the stars;
- experimenting with erosion by arranging sand and water in a water table;
- observing different terrains in the local area and then comparing the terrains to different areas (for example, valleys, hills, mountains, lakes).

Third Grade

2 Observes and describes simple changes in the earth and sky.

Active investigation of observable objects in the sky (clouds, sun, moon) leads third graders to understand that all objects in the sky (even those that require special tools to observe) have properties, locations, and movements that can be observed and described. They can explore different ways in which natural phenomena change the earth. Examples include:

- using a stream table to create erosion patterns on hills, then predicting a pattern on a higher hill;
- experimenting with a globe and flashlight to develop an explanation for the patterns of day and night;
- building a model of an earthquake and relating the effects produced by the model to pictures of the changes made by actual earthquakes;
- conducting an Internet search about the effects of acid rain on trees and soil;
- creating a scale model of the planets in the solar system;
- drawing accurate pictures of the constellations.

Social Studies

Encompassing history, economics, citizenship, and geography, the domain of social studies emphasizes social and cultural understanding. Children acquire this understanding from personal experiences and from the experiences of others. As children study present day and historical topics, they learn about human interdependence and the relationships between people and their environment. Throughout social studies, children use a variety of skills, including conducting research, using oral and visual sources, solving problems systematically, and making informed decisions using the democratic process.

Preschool-3

1 Begins to recognize own physical characteristics and those of others.

For three year olds, understanding culture begins with understanding themselves and their families. Three year olds combine their developing expertise in language with observations of themselves and those around them. They begin to identify their own physical attributes and point out—often in loud, clear language—the attributes of others. Children show growing awareness by:

- talking about details of similarity and difference, such as hair color and style;
- naming all the girls in the class, and adding, "and I'm one, too";
- imitating a deaf child's sign language and actually learning some signs;
- discussing food preferences with other children;
- asking about the different words Chinese- or Spanish-speaking classmates use when describing stories or events;
- noticing common physical attributes, such as two eyes, one nose, and two ears;
- announcing that they are girls, "and Kevin and Isaiah are boys."

Preschool-4

1 Identifies similarities and differences in personal and family characteristics.

Four year olds notice similarities and differences among themselves and others. Initially they focus on physical characteristics and family habits. With teacher guidance, they begin to show awareness that people are members of different cultural groups that have different habits, traditions, and customs. Examples include:

- coloring or painting an outline of themselves (body tracing) with colors of clothing and hair and eyes that match their own;
- looking at each person's skin and exploring the different colors and shades of each;
- noticing that some people speak differently than others and helping the teacher make a chart showing names of objects in two or three different languages;
- noting, "Tasha's family is different because she has two brothers and I have two sisters";
- talking about grandparents and discussing how they look different from children;
- enjoying different poems, songs, and stories about a variety of people.

Kindergarten

1 Identifies similarities and differences in people's characteristics, habits, and living patterns.

Five year olds develop self-identity by comparing themselves with others. At first, these comparisons focus on physical characteristics and preferences, but soon extend to recognizing similarities and differences within families or cultural groups. They continue to explore family roles and to examine other families to see how they differ from or are the same as their own. They learn about their classmates' cultures through conversations, dramatic play interactions, and items they bring to school from home. Examples include:

- exploring physical similarities and differences (such as, everyone has hair, but hair comes in different colors, textures, and lengths);
- exploring the language bilingual children speak at home and learning some words;
- tasting a snack that a classmate from another culture brings to school and exploring its relationship to holidays and other special occasions;
- looking at classmates' family photos and discussing the variety of family structures.

First Grade

1 Identifies similarities and differences in people's habits and living patterns.

First graders develop an appreciation for diversity by describing qualities that make individuals and families both unique and similar (for example, physical characteristics, personal interests, feelings, and ways of meeting basic human needs). They can begin to consider how membership in groups shapes people's lives in terms of family structure, language, foods, dress, conflict resolution methods, and celebrations. In this way they begin to gain an understanding of the meaning of culture. Evidence of their understanding includes:

- observing similarities and differences in self-portraits, photographs, and illustrations of different groups of people;
- constructing models of homes like those in their neighborhood;
- dramatizing scenes that reflect daily life and family habits;
- listening to a story and then mentioning that their family had to learn English when they moved here just like the family in the story;
- retelling a personal story about a family holiday celebration and comparing it to a story told by a peer.

Second Grade

1 Identifies similarities and differences in people's habits and living patterns.

Second graders recognize that people can be part of many different groups (family, classroom, culture, religion, community) and come from different backgrounds. They can identify many of the unique and shared qualities of people from diverse backgrounds and who lived in the recent past. By considering their own families and others in the community, they explore how membership in groups shapes people's lives (how it affects family structure, language, foods, dress, conflict resolution methods, celebrations). Examples include:

- bringing in objects from home (photo albums, family artifacts) that describe family habits;
- dramatizing scenes from a story to show how the daily living habits of children in Japan are similar and different from their own;
- relating personal experiences in their own family to those described in an historical fiction story;
- asking questions or offering opinions about a story in which the character's lifestyle is different from their own.

Third Grade

1 Identifies similarities and differences in habits and living patterns now and in the past.

Third graders recognize that all people have needs for government, education, transportation, communication, and recreation. They begin to explore similarities and differences in how people in different parts of the world meet these needs today and in times past. Through literature and research, they can contrast their own lives with those of others and come to understand that how people live and behave is often influenced by the groups to which they belong. Examples include:

- having a correspondence via e-mail with a pen pal in another country and comparing their in-school and after-school activities;
- charting similarities and differences between people living in their local region today as contrasted with two or three hundred years ago;
- writing a diary entry from the perspective of a famous explorer coming to a specific region three hundred years ago which describes the journey and what the explorer found upon arrival.

V Social Studies

A   People, past and present

Preschool-3	**Preschool-4**	**Kindergarten**

Preschool-3

Not expected at this level.

Preschool-4

Not expected at this level.

Kindergarten

2 Demonstrates beginning awareness of state and country.

In kindergarten, children begin to see themselves within a larger context. Their growing world includes not just their families and neighborhoods, but begins to extend to state and country. They recognize symbols of their own country and begin to develop an understanding of national holidays. They express their growing knowledge by:

- identifying an American flag while riding the bus to the apple orchard;

- explaining to a classmate why we celebrate George Washington's birthday;

- developing an awareness of some characteristics of their own region and, after seeing a snowstorm on television, commenting, "We never have snow where we live.";

- describing the White House as the place where the President lives;

- recognizing national figures who have changed our country (for example, Martin Luther King, Jr.).

V Social Studies

First Grade

2 Demonstrates beginning awareness about state and country.

First graders can begin to see themselves as part of their state's and nation's culture and heritage. Through literature, photographs, interviews, and discussions, they begin to identify symbols, events, places, customs and traditions that are important to their home state and country. Examples include:

- reading pictorial biographies of men and women who were important figures in American history;
- examining photographs of the region and noticing that almost every picture shows something related to farming;
- explaining to classmates why we celebrate various American holidays, such as Veterans Day, Memorial Day, or the Fourth of July;
- looking at a book about flags and identifying the American flag and the flag from their family's country of origin;
- drawing pictures of significant national buildings (the Capitol, the Statue of Liberty);
- using the name of their state and the word "state" correctly.

Second Grade

2 Demonstrates awareness about state and country.

Second graders can identify some symbols, events, places, and traditions that reflect the principles, goals, and customs of their own state and country. They can consider the physical and cultural characteristics of their region and begin to understand the historical significance of state and national landmarks. Some ways they express their developing understanding include:

- researching information about famous Americans using a variety of sources (for example, biographies, encyclopedias, photographs, CD-ROMs);
- knowing the words to patriotic songs;
- listing some of the ways people do things that are characteristic of their regions of the country (for example, ways of speaking, particular foods, sports teams);
- describing the history of an important national holiday (for example, Memorial Day, Presidents' Day);
- identifying significant local, state, and national buildings (the county courthouse, state capitol, White House).

Third Grade

2 Demonstrates awareness about state, region, and country.

Third graders can identify important symbols, events, places, and traditions that reflect the principles, goals, and customs of their own state, region, and country. They can understand the historical significance of state and national landmarks and important national documents. Some ways they express this developing understanding include:

- researching information about famous Americans (Benjamin Franklin, Father Miquel Hidalgo, Harriet Tubman) using a variety of sources (for example, biographies, encyclopedias, photographs, CD-ROMs);
- describing the history and meaning of important national documents (United States Constitution, Declaration of Independence);
- writing a research report about a famous explorer;
- describing the significance of regional ethnic and cultural celebrations;
- emulating the style of a famous local or regional historical artist or writer after studying examples of this person's work.

V Social Studies

Preschool-3

Not expected at this level.

Preschool-4

Not expected at this level.

Kindergarten

3 Shows some awareness of time and how the past influences people's lives.

Kindergartners learn about time by exploring calendar time and sequencing the events in their daily schedules. By reflecting on their own histories, they begin to learn about chronological time. Five year olds can use vocabulary related to chronology ("past," "present," "future," "before," "after," "yesterday," "today," "tomorrow"). They are beginning to understand that people in the past lived differently than people do today. Some ways children express this emerging historical understanding include:

- drawing and writing in a journal about a memory from preschool;
- explaining that people long ago used horses to travel because they didn't have cars;
- recounting the story of Harriet Tubman, indicating awareness of the past by beginning, "A long time ago....";
- making a timeline of their first five years of life;
- bringing family heirlooms to share with classmates (such as an oil lamp, a quilt, or a butter churn);
- telling a personal anecdote about the past in response to hearing a story read aloud.

First Grade

3 Shows beginning understanding of time and how the past influences people's lives.

First graders begin to demonstrate an understanding of chronological time as they learn to use such words as "yesterday," "tomorrow," "past," "present," and "future" accurately. When they hear stories of people in the past and learn about their own and classmates' family histories, they begin to understand that history tells the story of people and events from other times and places and that their lives are similar to and different from people's lives in the past. Some examples include:

- drawing and writing in a journal about the past or future (for example, a memory from preschool or a place they want to visit in the future);
- making a timeline of their first six years of life;
- using vocabulary related to chronology ("yesterday," "today," "tomorrow, "next year");
- retelling a story about the origin of a national holiday (for example, Lincoln's Birthday or Martin Luther King Day);
- interviewing grandparents to compare similarities and differences between life today and when their grandparents were growing up.

Second Grade

3 Shows some understanding of time and how the past influences people's lives.

By reflecting on their own history, second graders learn to differentiate between events that happened long ago and those that happened recently. Conversations and interviews with older relatives extend children's thinking about the past and their heritage. They can begin to consider how some things change with the passage of time and how the past affects life today. Examples include:

- collaborating with several other children to paint a mural depicting family life in their community long ago;
- making a timeline of their first seven years of life;
- writing a story that compares events in daily life with the way people lived long ago;
- listing sources of information that provide information about the past (interviews, museum trips, books, photographs);
- telling a story about an event in the past from the viewpoint of someone who lived through it;
- writing a research report about famous people in history and describing how their lives continue to affect life today.

Third Grade

3 Shows understanding of time and how the past influences people's lives.

Third graders can begin to understand how local, regional and national governments and their traditions have been shaped by events and people in history. They begin to understand cause and effect relationships, such as "Why did this happen in this way?" or "What might happen in the future?" They show their growing understanding of how the past shapes the present and the future by:

- making a timeline showing important events in the history of the local community and how these events affected people's lives;
- writing a paragraph that describes different historical events, using vocabulary that shows understanding of chronology (for example, "decade," "century");
- using a variety of resources (library books, Internet, photographs, museum visits) to gather information about the first settlers to the region, then organizing the information into chronological sequence and presenting it in writing with illustrations;
- reading biographies of well-known historical figures and dramatizing scenes from their lives.

Preschool-3

1 Begins to understand family structures and roles.

As three year olds engage in role-playing, they come to understand their own life experiences and learn about the roles of their family members. This understanding develops through concrete exploration during dramatic play, informal conversations, and "trying things out." Examples of how they explore roles include:

- pretending to nurture a doll by feeding and talking to it;
- adopting the roles of different family members when playing with other children in the dramatic play area;
- telling someone about a family routine, such as saying, "My uncle takes me for walks after supper";
- telling a classmate, "My big sister reads to me," and being amazed that the classmate does not have an older sister, but that the babysitter reads stories to him instead;
- bringing in a family photo and "introducing" each family member to the class.

Preschool-4

1 Begins to understand family needs, roles, and relationships.

Four year olds are very interested in learning about family roles and relationships. Through dramatic play and conversation, they actively explore the jobs family members perform to meet the family's needs (working, preparing dinner, driving the car, taking care of children). When they realize that a classmate's family structure differs from theirs, they want to explore those differences. Examples include:

- role-playing a variety of family members in the dramatic play area using words and/or actions;
- talking with the teacher or each other about when their mommies or grandpas go to work and what they do there;
- bringing in props from family members' work, such as hard hats, briefcases, or guitars, and using them during dramatic play;
- contributing to a class chart that lists each child, their family members, and the jobs each person does to help the rest of the family (shopping, cooking, cleaning, reading bedtime stories, washing clothes, taking out the trash, etc.).

Kindergarten

1 Begins to understand how people rely on others for goods and services.

Five year olds are learning to distinguish between wants and needs and are beginning to realize that making one choice means that you may not be able to do something else (for example, deciding to take a turn at the computer means you will not have time to build with blocks). Personal experience with making trades leads to a beginning awareness of money as a means to purchase goods and services. As their social world expands, children this age can begin to understand that all people need food, shelter, and clothing. Examples include:

- wondering aloud about how food gets to the grocery store;
- commenting that the class gerbil needs to eat every day just like people do;
- trading two pretzels for a friend's two crackers at snack time;
- realizing that when they made the choice to stay at the art area to finish their collage, they gave up their chance to play a lotto game;
- role playing a customer buying shoes in the classroom "shoe store," including looking at shoes, trying them on, making a decision, and exchanging money for the shoes.

First Grade

1 Recognizes some ways people rely on each other for goods and services.

First graders' emerging understanding of economics includes knowing that people fulfill their wants and needs by exchanging goods and services. They can identify examples of goods and services used in homes, schools, and communities and can describe different ways that people obtain them. As they begin to explore the role of money in exchange for goods and services, they learn about income, the meaning of "wants versus needs," and the consequences of wanting more than you can afford. Examples include:

- observing that the character in a story earns his living by working as a firefighter and asking who pays his salary;
- identifying and explaining choices families make when they go shopping for food;
- drawing and writing about service providers in the community (firefighters, mail carriers, police officers);
- making a list of all the supplies and materials needed to make the classroom run well;
- following a trip to the zoo, drawing and writing about the different jobs needed to run the zoo.

Second Grade

1 Recognizes some ways people rely on each other for goods and services.

Second graders can explain how a variety of goods and products are produced. As they explore community businesses and services today and in the past, they become more aware of the specialization of jobs and division of labor. They recognize the difference between producers and consumers and know that money must be earned before it can be used to purchase goods and services. They continue to explore the difference between needs and wants and the importance of making choices. Examples include:

- interviewing community workers in order to write a research report about the services they provide;
- participating in a discussion about how taxes pay for services such as libraries, schools, and parks;
- studying the produce section of the supermarket to determine which fruits and vegetables are produced locally and which come from other states or countries and then graphing the findings;
- creating a web of all the jobs involved in getting milk from a cow to the supermarket.

Third Grade

1 Shows some understanding of how people rely on each other for economic needs.

Third graders can consider ideas such as budgeting, scarcity, trade-offs, distribution, and supply and demand. They apply their understanding of these basic economic concepts to their studies of people in the past (for example, early American Indians, European settlers, pioneers) and present. Examples of how they show understanding include:

- sequencing and categorizing information from a variety of sources about the history of produce farming in their local region and then creating a graph or chart that depicts how farm products have changed over the last one hundred years;
- dramatizing scenes from historical fiction that depict how people bought, sold, and traded goods at outdoor markets long ago;
- participating in setting up a class newspaper and helping to create a scheme for division of labor;
- writing a research report about a famous explorer and describing who financed the exploration and why;
- writing up an interview with a small business owner.

Preschool-3

2 Describes some jobs that people do.

Employment is still a rather abstract idea for most three year olds, as are the roles adult family members fill in their workplaces. They may be able to name a parent's job (nurse, plumber, farmer), but may not know what parents actually do at those jobs. However, visiting a grocery store, going to the library, or watching a bridge repair crew at work help three year olds learn about the world of work. Children show their growing awareness of their community by:

- pretending to be a grocery store clerk in dramatic play;
- requesting a hard hat so that they can "fix" the pretend road made of blocks;
- looking at the picture book about someone going to the shoe store or the bakery;
- describing a visit to a parent's workplace;
- grabbing a briefcase in dramatic play and saying, "Goodbye. I'm going to work," then simply wandering around the classroom.

Preschool-4

2 Describes some people's jobs and what is required to perform them.

In addition to understanding family roles, four year olds are also interested in knowing more about the community members they encounter in their lives. With encouragement, they will expand their interest beyond firefighters and police officers to include storekeepers, postal workers, nurses, doctors, garbage collectors, road builders, and others. They can identify a variety of common jobs, give simple explanations about what workers do, and identify some tools used to perform specific jobs. Examples include:

- experimenting with a cash register, postal scale, stethoscope, or other occupational tools in dramatic play;
- acting out in dramatic play how the shoe salesperson helps you buy shoes;
- using the flannel board to recall a trip to an orchard, and showing how apples are picked and packed;
- looking at books to identify the various machines used for road construction;
- asking for props to role play a community worker (a firefighter's hat or a police officer's whistle and white gloves).

Kindergarten

2 Describes some people's jobs and what is required to perform them.

Five year olds are ready to examine their communities and explore the many roles people fill in helping each other live. They have a beginning understanding of why people have jobs and can identify different types of jobs and some of the tools used to perform those jobs. They show this growing knowledge by:

- taking on the role of a salesperson or mail carrier, involving others in this play, and asking questions about the way these jobs are performed and what tools each uses;
- pretending to be a police officer, discussing why police officers are necessary, and exploring their many roles;
- contributing to a mural about the people in the school and the jobs they do;
- pretending to be their own father or mother going to work outside the home and acting out what they do on their jobs;
- expressing through the arts (dramatic play, music, painting, blocks) the role of a community worker, including descriptions of the tools needed to do the job.

First Grade

2 Shows some understanding of the specialized nature of the work people do.

As first graders explore community businesses and services (local stores, the fire station, or a farm), they can explain the requirements of various jobs and how specialized jobs contribute to the production of goods and services. Through active research, they begin to recognize how each job serves specific functions, requires specialized training, and makes use of particular tools, equipment, and machinery. Children demonstrate this understanding by:

- creating a diner in the classroom and taking on the roles of cook, server, cashier, and customer;

- making a mural of the people who work in the supermarket, complete with details about how they do their jobs;

- drawing and writing a story about bread-making equipment based on a trip to the local bakery;

- creating a chart listing the names of many different jobs in the neighborhood, the equipment used in each job, and the tasks the workers perform;

- building an assembly line out of Legos after a trip to an automobile factory.

Second Grade

See the following indicator on page 139 in Social Studies:

B Human interdependence

1 Recognizes some ways people rely on each other for goods and services.

See the following indicator on page 143 in Social Studies:

B Human interdependence

2 Identifies some ways technology influences people's lives.

Third Grade

See the following indicator on page 139 in Social Studies:

B Human interdependence

1 Shows some understanding of how people rely on each other for economic needs.

See the following indicator on page 143 in Social Studies:

B Human interdependence

2 Shows understanding of the influence of technology on people's lives now and in the past.

V Social Studies

Preschool-3	Preschool-4	Kindergarten

Preschool-3

Not expected at this level.

Preschool-4

3 **Begins to be aware of technology and how it affects life.**

Surrounded by TVs, ovens, computers, planes, and automated machinery, four year olds are aware of technology in their environment. As teachers talk with them, children can begin to appreciate that they would not know about events in other places without radios and TVs and could not talk to or visit distant relatives so easily without telephones, cars or planes. For four year olds, examples of their awareness of technology include:

• using the tape player to listen to a story in the Listening Center;

• describing the nature program about giraffes in Africa that they watched on TV;

• sharing during circle time that "Grandma called from Puerto Rico to say happy birthday";

• looking at X-rays in the dramatic play area brought in as a prop for the Dentist's Office or Hospital;

• exploring multimedia effects on the computer.

Kindergarten

3 **Begins to be aware of technology and how it affects life.**

Five year olds are very interested in the technology that is so much a part of the world around them (television, telephones, vehicles, video games, VCRs, microwave ovens, computers). They can discuss ways in which technology helps people accomplish specific tasks and, with teacher guidance, consider what it must have been like to live without technology in an earlier time. Examples of how children show an understanding of how technology influences their lives include:

• visiting the bread factory and upon returning to the classroom, recreating the machines they observed using Legos, unit blocks, or Tinker Toys;

• using the class computer to play a math game;

• role playing preparing a family dinner using the kitchen appliances in the dramatic play area;

• using a Polaroid camera to take a photo of their block building;

• beginning to use computers for word processing.

First Grade

3 **Identifies some ways technology influences people's lives.**

First graders can begin to recognize various kinds of tools and technology and how they help people do things better. They identify forms of technology used in everyday life (cars, bridges, televisions, computers, stoves, VCRs) and describe ways these affect our lives (communicating, traveling long distances, watching TV, playing computer games). Examples include:

- sharing ideas in a group discussion about potential future means of communication;
- describing household tools and appliances and how they make family life easier;
- drawing and writing about how people traveled from place to place before present day forms of transportation (cars, buses, trains, and planes) were available;
- learning about an inventor at home (perhaps by using a CD-ROM with an older sibling) and sharing the information with the class;
- constructing a complex highway system in the block area;
- creating an invention in the classroom through the use of found materials;
- using the word processor to keep records about science projects.

Second Grade

2 **Identifies some ways technology influences people's lives.**

Second graders are becoming increasingly interested in how technology affects people's jobs, leisure activities, and their knowledge of faraway places. They can describe some ways in which devices people have designed (for communication, transportation, information organization, etc.) make life easier or more difficult today than in the past. Examples of how they do this include:

- reading a story about an inventor or famous scientist and telling the class about it;
- making a graph on the computer showing different methods of transportation families use to get to school and work;
- coming up with a problem and trying to invent a device to solve it;
- watching a video about how dams are constructed and then making a drawing of a dam;
- imagining life in their town before telephones were invented and writing a story about how local news was communicated;
- comparing the features of an old car with a new car and then designing a "car of the future."

Third Grade

2 **Shows understanding of the influence of technology on people's lives now and in the past.**

As third graders learn about continuity and change over time, they can reflect on how technology has changed and the impact of such change on people's lives around the world. They also have some knowledge of famous scientists and inventors. Examples of how third graders express this understanding include:

- reading biographies of famous inventors and making a presentation about the impact of their work on our lives;
- presenting a research report to the class about important scientists and how their discoveries changed their own lives and the lives of others (for example, Louis Pasteur, Marie Curie, George Washington Carver);
- making a chart comparing current farm equipment to that of the past and how particular equipment affects the lives and economy in their own community and region;
- making a drawing of the first television set or of early computers and writing a report describing some ways these inventions have affected the economy.

V Social Studies

Preschool-3

1 **Shows awareness of group rules.**

At three, children are beginning to learn about how to behave in groups. They do not yet understand the reasons for rules. Although they might be able to repeat rules, they cannot follow them consistently without adult help. Showing a beginning awareness of rules includes:

- chanting that it's time to clean up while continuing to play;
- riding a tricycle only in the specified area of the playground;
- waiting patiently with coat and hat on because the rule is that everyone needs to be ready before anyone goes outside;
- participating in word and song games that have rules (for example, "Ring Around the Rosie");
- verbalizing that there is no hitting other people in this classroom because hitting hurts;
- participating actively in class clean-up time.

Preschool-4

1 **Demonstrates awareness of rules.**

Four year olds can be very strict about adhering to classroom rules. They like having clear rules and prefer that rules be followed. They can begin to understand, with guidance, why rules are important for cooperative living. They show an understanding of rules by:

- helping to make the rules for free choice (for example, only four people at the sand table) and beginning to understand why such rules are helpful;
- following rules on the playground, such as no bumping into people when you are on the tricycle or your "license" will be taken away;
- accepting that they have to wait before painting because the easels are full;
- explaining to a classmate why the hamster cannot be taken out of its cage;
- stating the "no hitting" rule;
- using a personal symbol or name tag to save a place at an interest area.

Kindergarten

1 **Demonstrates awareness of the reasons for rules.**

Children's understanding of the reasons for rules and laws comes about as they discuss problems in the classroom and school and participate in making reasonable rules that directly involve them. They demonstrate their understanding of rules and laws by showing such positive citizenship behaviors as sharing, taking turns, following rules, and taking responsibility for classroom jobs. Ways that children reveal their understanding of the need for rules include:

- explaining classroom rules to a classmate;
- helping to set the rules for the number of children playing at the sand table and discussing why the rules were made and what could happen if the rules aren't followed;
- incorporating into their play the reasons for traffic signs and symbols (such as red and green traffic lights, solid and broken highway lines, stop signs) and the role of crossing guards and police officers;
- exploring various family rules ("What are some rules in each family?" "How many families have rules that are like rules in other families?").

First Grade

1 **Demonstrates some understanding of the reasons for rules and laws.**

Children's understanding of the reasons for rules, laws, and active citizenship is strengthened as they practice responsible behavior, respond to others respectfully, discuss everyday problems in the classroom and school, and participate in formulating reasonable rules. First graders can explain the need for basic rules and laws, why people want to be treated fairly, and that certain rules help make this possible. They are beginning to understand how voting is used to make choices and decisions. Ways that children reveal this understanding include:

- helping to establish classroom rules and explaining why certain rules are fair or unfair;
- mediating a conflict over a game rule;
- providing some examples of traffic laws in the community and the symbols of these laws that keep people safe (stop signs, traffic lights, crosswalks);
- participating in group discussions about rules and laws in the community (for example, considering why there are traffic rules and anti-shoplifting laws);
- making a list of characteristics describing a good citizen.

Second Grade

1 **Demonstrates understanding of the reasons for rules and laws.**

Children's understanding of the reasons for rules, laws, and responsible citizenship grows as they practice responsible behavior, respond respectfully to others, discuss everyday problems in the classroom and school, and participate in creating reasonable rules. Second graders begin to understand why countries make laws to maintain order, preserve people's rights, and establish consequences for breaking laws. They can begin to describe how groups resolve conflicts. Ways that children reveal this understanding include:

- helping to set classroom rules;
- explaining the reasons for laws in the community;
- reacting to incidents of unfairness or injustice portrayed in the news or in stories;
- conducting a survey of children and adults about why laws should exist;
- participating in a discussion about the difference between voting and coming to consensus as a way of making a decision;
- helping peers mediate a conflict.

Third Grade

1 **Shows some understanding of how rules and laws help protect people and property.**

Eight year olds' understanding of the reasons for rules and laws is apparent in their discussions of everyday problems in the classroom and school and in their formulation of reasonable rules. They can consider ways in which rules and laws protect people's rights and ensure that people are treated fairly. They can begin to compare how laws are made and upheld today as compared with earlier times. Some examples of how third graders express this understanding include:

- participating in group discussion about fair and equal pay for men and women;
- reading about how the United States Constitution was written;
- writing in a journal about why communities need rules and laws to function;
- writing a research report about how laws were upheld in this country's early settlements;
- reading biographies of famous Americans who fought for freedom (for example, Abraham Lincoln, Cèsar Chávez, Martin Luther King, Jr.).

V Social Studies

145

Preschool-3

Not expected at this level.

Preschool-4

2 **Shows awareness of what it means to be a leader.**

The role of a leader is an abstract concept. At this age, many children are only able to address the concrete leadership roles they experience. This includes the teacher's role and, possibly, the principal's or director's role. Four year olds may also show some awareness of the leadership qualities that parents or caregivers exhibit. Children show their interest in leadership by:

- pretending to be the band director or conductor when playing with musical instruments;
- pretending to be the teacher during dramatic play;
- choosing a leader for the block building project and then talking about what this means as they work together;
- trying to figure out who is the "boss" of the firehouse or the police station after a visit;
- talking to the principal or the director about his or her job;
- showing some leadership qualities as they pretend to be parents or caretakers during dramatic play.

Kindergarten

2 **Shows beginning understanding of what it means to be a leader.**

By five, children show some awareness of leadership in their classrooms and schools. They can understand the important roles that the teacher and principal play in making things run in an orderly way. Five year olds can participate in assigning leadership roles for various class activities. Their understanding of leadership expands as they identify the leaders in their community (the police chief, the mayor) and the functions they perform. Examples include:

- playing fire chief in the dramatic play area and deciding what the chief has to do that is different from other fire fighters;
- talking with peers about the job of a person "in charge" during snack or circle time;
- taking responsibility for classroom jobs such as line leader, plant waterer, or name tag collector;
- deciding to be the leader for the block building that is about to get started;
- making a book about the things done by a particular leader in school or the community.

First Grade

2 Shows understanding of what it means to be a good leader.

Six year olds have a beginning understanding of what it means to be a classroom leader. Learning about leaders in their schools and communities (principal, town council member, police chief) helps them consider the role of authority figures, the qualities of good leadership, how good leaders help groups function effectively, and the ways that leaders are selected. They show their beginning understanding of leadership by:

- assuming positive leadership roles in games and projects;

- observing how a story character showed leadership qualities;

- telling the class that their family has a sign for a candidate on their lawn to help the candidate get elected to town council;

- sharing information from an interview with the principal about her job;

- suggesting that the class vote to determine the guinea pig's name.

Second Grade

2 Shows beginning understanding of government functions.

Children aged seven have some understanding of what it means to be a classroom leader, and fair decision-making is very important to them. By gaining familiarity with leaders in their community (principal, town council member, mayor), they can consider the qualities of good leadership, how good leaders help groups function effectively, how leaders are selected or elected, and how decisions are made in a democracy. They demonstrate their beginning understanding of government by:

- suggesting compromise or voting as a way to settle a disagreement;

- gathering information from the Internet about the role of elected officials (for example, the mayor or governor) and then reporting it to the class;

- discussing a simple community issue;

- interviewing a local community leader about how municipal decisions are made;

- listing reasons why a good leader should possess certain qualities.

Third Grade

2 Shows some understanding of government functions.

Third graders are learning about the basic structure and function of local government. They need time and practice to learn what makes a good leader and how fair decisions are made. By reading stories about historical times or other cultures, third graders can reflect on why different groups had different ways of handling decisions. Some ways third graders demonstrate their emerging understanding in this area include:

- describing how they would address a local issue if they were elected to local office;

- creating a chart that shows the function of different parts of local community government;

- role-playing an election debate;

- researching various forms of community government and comparing strengths and weaknesses;

- comparing and contrasting aspects of the school's student government with the local government and school board.

V Social Studies

Preschool-3

Not expected at this level.

Preschool-4

1 **Describes the location of things in the environment.**

Understanding the concept of location provides the foundation for geographic thinking. Four year olds show they understand location by placing objects in specific positions in the surrounding environment or noticing how objects are spatially related to one another ("The yellow house is very far away."). They can become quite enthusiastic about matching objects to their usual geographic locations (a toaster in the kitchen, a bed in the bedroom, a tree in the park). Examples include:

• placing pictures of common household items in the proper rooms of a prepared house floor plan and explaining why they go there;

• using the teacher's clue that "The markers are below the pencils" to locate the markers on the shelf;

• talking about the stores they visit and what is in them;

• using a flannel board to show the order of stores on their main street;

• following a simple treasure hunt map within the classroom.

Kindergarten

1 **Expresses beginning geographic thinking.**

For five year olds, geographical thinking begins with deepening their understanding of the concept of location. They can move their bodies in specific directions, describe the relative locations of objects, and talk about location using appropriate vocabulary such as "near," "far," "over," "under," and "next to." Learning that real places can be represented symbolically occurs as children make drawings, build with blocks, and create models of real places. Examples include:

• building a familiar street with blocks and positioning homes and stores in proper order;

• following a picture map to the treasure the teacher has hidden on the playground;

• playing a game in which they move from place to place according to specific directions;

• talking about how long it took to drive to a grandparent's house in another state;

• locating objects in the room by drawing a map of the classroom which shows the windows, tables, and activity and interest areas;

• pointing to the blue areas on a map or globe and asking for confirmation that these show water.

First Grade

1 Shows beginning understanding that maps represent actual places.

Six year olds are still working at understanding that real places can be represented symbolically on maps. They can create and read pictorial maps, locate significant places on a map or globe (their own community, state, and country), and begin to consider the reasons for the locations of communities and places within communities. Some ways children demonstrate their understanding of maps include:

• making a blueprint or diagram of a block structure;

• showing the class some of the maps their families used on their vacations to help them get from place to place;

• finding the directional key on a map of the neighborhood and using north, south, east, and west to describe familiar locations;

• using a map to identify the location of places in the community and explaining why they are located where they are;

• finding their own state and country on a globe;

• making a map of the playground.

Second Grade

1 Uses simple mapping skills.

Creating flat and 3-D maps of actual places they have seen firsthand helps deepen second graders' understanding that maps are symbolic representations of real places. They can create maps that include symbols, a directional key, legends, and a title. They can also learn about other mapping symbols. At seven, children demonstrate their understanding of maps by:

• creating a map to show a safe route from their homes to the school;

• making maps of their classrooms, bedrooms, or playgrounds, and labeling them;

• locating places in the community on a simple letter-number grid system map;

• using the scale of miles on a road map to estimate distance;

• using different symbols to represent real places on a map and creating a legend;

• locating significant places (for example, states, countries, oceans, continents) on a world map or globe.

Third Grade

1 Uses maps to organize information about people and their environment.

Third graders can make, read, and interpret maps. They have a beginning understanding of scale and can read and create legends on maps. They demonstrate their understanding of maps by:

• constructing models of communities or cities that show specific geographical features of a local area (for example, deserts, mountains, oceans, rivers);

• using maps, charts, and photographs to classify regions with common characteristics;

• making maps and using symbols (of the local environment, imaginary places, or story settings);

• drawing a map, to scale and with a legend, of the area where the school is located;

• making models that express geographical features (rivers, mountains);

• using globes, atlases, and maps as resources to describe the geographic features of the community;

• drawing aerial representations of a town, city, or state;

• locating important state and national sites on a classroom map.

V Social Studies

Preschool-3

1 Shows beginning awareness of their environment.

Three year olds show awareness of their environment by first noticing features of their homes and other familiar places. Over time, their curiosity about place extends to their neighborhoods. They comment on changes and inquire about unfamiliar items. With guided observations from adults, three year olds can become aware that sometimes people do things that affect the environment in a negative way. Leaving too many toys on the rug, for example, makes it difficult to have circle time. These preschoolers show their awareness of the environment by:

- helping to bring in playground toys so they will not get wet if it rains;
- explaining to a classmate, "We have to pick up the paper from the floor and throw it in the trash basket";
- telling the teacher about the water flowing over the road on the way to school;
- helping to wipe off the table after a painting project "to make it all clean";
- discussing ways their families help keep their neighborhood clean or safe;
- helping to take cans, bottles, and paper to the recycling center.

Preschool-4

2 Shows awareness of the environment.

Interest in the environment is very concrete for four year old children. Initially they notice major changes in their environment. With teacher support, they can begin to understand how people affect the environment by relating it to the classroom and to their own yards and neighborhoods. They show a growing understanding by:

- noticing new displays or materials in the classroom;
- sharing information about the progress of the road repairs they saw on their way to school;
- discussing reasons for not picking flowers on the walk they recently took;
- explaining to a classmate why a passageway must be kept uncluttered for visually and physically impaired classmates;
- discussing how the classroom would look if everyone dropped tissues on the floor or didn't wash the table after finger painting;
- talking about why it would be hard to play with the blocks if they were all over the classroom, rather than in one place.

Kindergarten

2 Shows beginning awareness of the relationship between people and where they live.

Five year olds are developing an awareness of their local environment. They can describe some physical characteristics (for example, bodies of water, mountains, weather) and some of the human characteristics of their communities (types of shelter, clothing, food, jobs). With repeated exposure to different places, they begin to notice the physical and human characteristics of other places. With teacher guidance and support, they recognize how people can take care of or damage the world around them. Children show this beginning understanding by:

- noticing different types of houses on a walk around the neighborhood;
- commenting that the child in the story about Alaska needed a very warm winter coat;
- painting pictures of what they see out of the classroom window;
- recycling lunch containers and other paper products used during the day and discussing what happens when these waste products are thrown in the trash bins.

First Grade

2 Begins to identify ways the environment affects how people live and work.

Six year olds are developing an awareness of the physical and human characteristics of their environment. They can describe some physical features of where they live (for example, near the ocean or in the mountains) and begin to explore differences between how they and others live. They can begin to make connections that show how the climate and physical features of their environment affect the way people live and work. Some ways children reveal this understanding include:

- constructing detailed models of their local environment;

- drawing or painting pictures that reflect an understanding of the community's physical features;

- offering a logical explanation during a group discussion about why many community jobs are related to snow removal or hurricane protection;

- comparing the weather described in a story with that of their community;

- talking about ways that housing reflects particular locations.

Second Grade

2 Identifies ways the environment affects how people live and work.

Second graders can make connections between how the climate, physical features, and natural resources of the environment affect people's jobs, clothing, housing, and foods. They can understand why people rely on the natural resources of their local environment to meet basic needs. Some ways children reveal this understanding include:

- constructing models, drawing pictures, or making paintings that detail the natural (for example, mountains and rivers) and human features (houses, buildings, and roads) of the local environment;

- comparing a rural and urban community to see similarities and differences in housing and transportation;

- speculating, based on knowledge of the physical features and natural resources of the community, how people living in the community a long time ago may have built their houses and gotten their food;

- writing a research report describing the natural features of their community and how these affect daily life.

Third Grade

2 Identifies ways the environment affects how people live and work.

Third graders can identify different ways people's lives are affected by their environment (for example, climate, physical features, and natural resources). Whether studying the local community or a place far away or in the past, they can reflect on how environmental factors, including natural resources, have shaped the culture, traditions, and economy of communities. Examples include:

- constructing models, drawing pictures, or making paintings that detail how people used the natural resources of a region over time;

- writing a research report about how houses in a bayou are constructed and why, then comparing this construction to the way houses are made in a different region;

- observing how an author has shaped a story's action by incorporating features of the physical environment;

- comparing transportation methods in different regions of the country based on climate and natural resources;

- researching how people in different parts of the country use leisure time and explaining how the environment might affect leisure activities.

V Social Studies

Preschool-3

See the following indicator on page 150 in Social Studies:

D People and where they live

1 Shows beginning awareness of their environment.

Preschool-4

See the following indicator on page 150 in Social Studies:

D People and where they live

1 Shows awareness of their environment.

Kindergarten

See the following indicator on page 150 in Social Studies:

D People and where they live

2 Shows beginning awareness of the relationship between people and where they live.

First Grade

3 Begins to recognize how people affect their environment.

Through projects and discussions, six year olds can begin to think about how people use the resources in their environment to meet basic needs. They can identify some ways that people change the environment (building roads and houses, cutting down trees, polluting water) and begin to recognize some reasons to protect and conserve natural resources. Children demonstrate their understanding through such concrete actions as:

- remembering to use classroom recycling bins;
- drawing and writing about ways to protect the forest after interviewing a conservation officer, naturalist, or environmentalist;
- participating in a discussion about water conservation and suggesting that children in the classroom turn off the faucet while they are soaping their hands;
- making references to environmental concerns in a journal entry or during puppet plays, skits, or dramatic play with blocks;
- picking up litter on the playground and putting it in the trash.

Second Grade

3 Recognizes how people affect their environment.

As seven year olds become more aware of how people change their environment for specific purposes (such as building highways, cutting down trees, and burning coal), they can think about the positive and negative effects of these actions. Some ways second graders demonstrate this understanding include:

- reminding classmates to use classroom recycling bins;
- expressing concern during class discussions about environmental issues (for example, recycling and water pollution);
- generating some ideas about how to conserve natural resources in the community;
- drawing pictures of how the town landscape might have looked at an earlier time and proposing explanations for why it changed.

Third Grade

3 Recognizes how people affect their environment.

By the time students are in third grade, they can be expected to think about how people have changed the environment for specific purposes (such as building dams, bridges, highways, and skyscrapers). As they explore the positive and negative effects of these changes, they gain an awareness of how they can contribute to preserving the earth's natural resources. Examples of this understanding include:

- showing concern for pollution (participating in discussions, initiating a classroom recycling project, bringing in news articles about toxic waste in a local river);
- writing a research report about factories along the local river and how their presence has affected the people and the environment;
- writing an article for the school newspaper about recycling;
- learning about the causes of global warming and comparing average winter and summer temperatures in their area from research on the Web.

V Social Studies

The Arts

The emphasis in this domain is on children's engagement with the arts (dance, dramatics, music, and fine arts), both actively and receptively, rather than mastery of skills and techniques related to particular artistic media. The components address two ideas: how children use the arts to express, represent, and integrate their experiences, and how children develop an understanding and appreciation for the arts. It focuses on how opportunities to use and appreciate the arts enable children to demonstrate what they know, expand their thinking, and make connections among the arts, culture, history, and other domains.

Preschool-3

1 Participates in group music experiences.

Three year olds eagerly participate in large and small group music activities. They can carry a simple tune and remember some words to songs and finger plays. They can participate in rhythm bands, but have trouble integrating several activities at once, such as singing and playing a rhythm instrument simultaneously. Their participation includes:

- joining in songs during circle time, engaging in a song's hand motions, and remembering the words to an oft-repeated song;
- suggesting words for open-ended songs, such as "Aiken Drum," or suggesting animals for "Old MacDonald";
- galloping or marching in time to the music, slowing down or speeding up when the rhythm changes;
- asking to sing a particular song at circle time;
- trying different ways to make sounds with triangles or cymbals;
- using rhythm sticks, drums, or tambourines in time to the music.

Preschool-4

1 Participates in group music experiences.

Four year olds quickly become involved in singing, finger plays, chants, musical instruments, and moving to music. They are usually quite unselfconscious when participating in music activities and can gain a sense of mastery if there are no expected outcomes or performances. Examples of involvement include:

- participating in finger plays and musical games;
- listening to music tapes during choice time;
- starting and stopping the playing of their instruments when the piano or tape starts or stops;
- knowing the words of oft-repeated songs, humming or singing them during other parts of the day;
- using rhythm sticks or other instruments in time to a beat;
- making up songs to accompany their play activities;
- clapping hands in time to a song or a record, or copying the clapping beat of the teacher.

Kindergarten

1 Participates in group music experiences.

Five year olds are able to master simple instruments, such as rhythm sticks, tambourines, or drums. They are interested in the sounds that more complicated instruments (for example, a piano or guitar) make and in how they are played. They enjoy singing, making up silly and rhyming verses, imitating rhythmic patterns, learning finger plays, and using music to tell stories and express feelings. Often, they will make up songs to accompany other activities such as when playing on the swings or putting on their clothes to go outside. Examples of music participation include:

- singing songs from different cultures;
- clapping to the beat of a song or tape;
- exploring musical instruments that are in the classroom and using common objects to produce a variety of sounds;
- composing their own songs and singing as they perform classroom routines, wait in line, or use the swings;
- using musical instruments to create a mood to go along with a puppet show or a creative dance.

First Grade

1 Explores materials and techniques in the arts.

Exposure to different media and techniques enables six year olds to experiment with different ways to use visual arts media, construction (blocks and other building materials), music, dance, and dramatics. Familiarity and experience contribute to their understanding of and ability to use different art media and art forms with flexibility and inventiveness. Some ways first graders explore the arts include:

- creating intricate structures using blocks, Legos, or other building materials;
- creating sculptures or constructions using recycled materials;
- creating collages using more than two media;
- using several musical instruments to create many different sounds;
- experimenting with different ways to mix colors of paint to get realistic skin tones;
- learning the words to the songs sung in the classroom or at an assembly;
- moving to music by hopping, leaping, and skipping.

Second Grade

1 Explores materials and techniques in the arts.

Familiarity and experience help second graders experiment with different media related to the visual arts, music, dance, and drama. When given opportunities, second graders participate in arts experiences and use artistic materials and processes purposefully. For second graders, examples of this include:

- creating sculptures using found materials;
- using paints and brushes in experimental ways to create texture in a painting;
- creating 2- and 3-D constructions with blocks, Legos, or found objects (wood scraps, corks, Styrofoam, etc.);
- using a variety of musical instruments to create sound effects;
- learning the words to songs or making up new verses.

Third Grade

1 Experiments with new ideas, materials, and processes in the arts.

Students grow artistically by exploring a variety of sophisticated materials and techniques. When given the opportunity to choose materials or processes with which to explore the arts, third graders demonstrate increased skills and perseverance. Examples include:

- hearing a song and making up a new series of verses;
- experimenting with tempo and volume in a musical composition;
- experimenting with drawing software;
- making up a dance to a popular musical selection;
- experimenting with texture using clay or papier-maché until they achieve the effect they are looking for;
- inventing new brush techniques when painting.

VI The Arts

Preschool-3

2 Participates in creative movement, dance, and drama.

Three year olds enjoy moving, playing, and creating with their bodies. They are ready to use dance and other movement to express feelings that would be difficult for them to express verbally. They experiment with creative ways to move and take on roles that enable them to act out very simple stories. Examples include:

- crawling, "flying," walking on tip toe, or performing almost any other imaginative movement in response to music;
- acting out how they fell off the tricycle while going very fast around a corner on the playground;
- using scarves in a free movement, floating them overhead or twirling them around;
- galloping, twirling, bending, and stretching to music;
- imitating animals such as butterflies or elephants;
- responding with bodily, facial, and arm movements to the moods and rhythms of different types of music.

Preschool-4

2 Participates in creative movement, dance, and drama.

Four year olds can participate with abandon in dancing and creative movement. Their imaginations are overflowing with images and ideas that they can express with movement. They pantomime movement of familiar things, act out stories, and re-enact events from their own lives in dramatic play. Examples include:

- using scarves, ribbons, or other materials to create special movements and dances;
- dramatizing a story read aloud during circle time;
- using movement to interpret or imitate feelings, animals, and such things as plants growing or a rain storm;
- dancing to a variety of different kinds of music, such as jazz, rock, ethnic, classical;
- galloping, twirling, and "flying," or performing almost any other imaginative movement in response to music;
- acting out the role of the mother in dramatic play;
- creating innovative movements to accompany audio tapes or group singing.

Kindergarten

2 Participates in creative movement, dance, and drama.

Five year olds are very active and need opportunities to move and stretch their bodies. They are in constant motion, wiggling, changing positions, and sitting in a variety of ways. They can harness this energy into creative and descriptive expressions of feelings and experiences through movement, dance, and drama. Examples include:

- participating in a group movement experience and suggesting ways to move and animals to imitate;
- planning or joining with others in the dramatization of a book or the retelling of a class event;
- pantomiming the actions of a leaf falling, a ball bouncing, or a bird flying;
- dramatizing a story they created;
- making up a drama about something they studied or visited, such as a circus or a trip to the zoo;
- creating a movement that responds to the beat of a record or interpreting the mood conveyed by a classical composition.

First Grade

See the following indicator on page 161 in The Arts:

A   Expression and representation

2   Uses the arts to express and represent ideas, experiences, and emotions.

Second Grade

See the following indicator on page 161 in The Arts:

A   Expression and representation

2   Uses the arts to express and represent ideas, experiences, and emotions.

Third Grade

See the following indicator on page 161 in The Arts:

A   Expression and representation

2   Uses the arts to express and represent ideas, experiences, and emotions.

Preschool-3

3 Uses a variety of art materials for tactile experience and exploration.

Three year olds enjoy the flexibility and control that comes with using the wide range of art materials available in the classroom. Many children like being "messy" in a controlled situation, while others work hard to keep clean. At this age, their motivations are exploration, pleasure, and discovery, not the end products that might result from their efforts. Examples of their efforts include:

- trying one medium many times in order to experience its properties in depth (such as painting at the easel several days in a row, using several colors, or covering the whole paper with paint);

- constructing a flat structure with unit blocks, randomly exchanging pieces until they feel satisfied;

- punching, patting, rolling, squishing, and flattening play dough;

- using a variety of drawing materials, such as markers, pencils, chalk, and crayons;

- messing about with finger paint or colored shaving cream, making many different swirls and dabs.

Preschool-4

3 Uses a variety of art materials for tactile experience and exploration.

Four year olds are very active, and can sustain attention to art activities for only limited periods of time. They engage in the artistic process with great enthusiasm, but show little desire to produce a product. This enables them to explore various media with freedom. They demonstrate exploration by:

- trying a variety of materials and ways of using the materials (for example, using a big brush to paint broad strokes, single lines going this way and that, or combining colors);

- experimenting with play dough by rolling and patting it, cutting it with cookie cutters, sticking things into it, or sometimes making it into an object;

- drawing or otherwise creating backdrops for puppet shows or signs for block structures;

- using new implements, such as Q-tips or straws, to paint a picture;

- constructing a symmetrical design with pattern blocks;

- using chalk on the blackboard or on paper;

- using stamps or other objects to print with paint or ink.

Kindergarten

3 Uses a variety of art materials to explore and express ideas and emotions.

Through extensive exploration with art materials, five year olds become confident using a variety of media and enhance their sense of mastery and creativity. Although they are primarily interested in the creative process, they are beginning to become more critical of the products they create. They can express their feelings and ideas through their art work, in addition to expressing them verbally. Examples of exploration and expression with art materials include:

- trying a variety of expressive media (markers, brush and finger painting, printing, collage, play dough, clay);

- drawing or painting the way they feel when they are happy;

- making a book with their own pictures to illustrate a story they dictated;

- using one medium for a period of time to develop greater control and expertise;

- constructing a sculpture from wood pieces, fabric, and foil;

- creating an object or animal with clay.

First Grade

2 Uses the arts to express and represent ideas, experiences, and emotions.

The arts are an effective way for children to recreate and make sense of their experiences. When given opportunities, six year olds can initiate and invent ways to connect and apply the arts in assignments, projects, and presentations across the curriculum. They use drawing, painting, dramatization, music, dance, and construction as tools to convey thoughts and ideas. For first graders, examples of this include:

- creating a visual representation of an object, place, or event (for example, painting a picture of the firehouse after a class visit or constructing a model bridge using straws, Popsicle sticks, cardboard, and aluminum foil);
- using musical instruments to express an interpretation of a story or poem;
- finding innovative ways to use collage and construction materials (rug samples, Styrofoam, pieces of wood, wallpaper samples) to build a realistic model of the inside of a house;
- using many different materials to create detailed puppets and puppet show scenery to represent a scene for a story;
- inventing a playful song with rhyming words.

Second Grade

2 Uses the arts to express and represent ideas, experiences, and emotions.

The arts are an effective way for children to recreate and make sense of their learning across the curriculum. Seven year olds can initiate and plan increasingly detailed representations of objects, actions, and events, as well as ideas and emotions using the visual arts, dance, drama, and music. Examples of how second graders demonstrate these abilities include:

- creating a visual representation of an object, place, or event (for example, painting a self-portrait or creating an animal with clay);
- making a diorama of an animal's habitat;
- duplicating intricate architectural structures from their cities or states using blocks, Legos, and other building materials;
- using musical instruments to express an interpretation of a story or poem;
- creating intricate pattern designs using colored pencils and graph paper;
- dramatizing a scene from a story.

Third Grade

2 Uses the arts to express and represent ideas, experiences, and emotions.

The arts are an effective way for students to re-create and make sense of their learning across the curriculum. Third graders can explore relationships among the arts and other subjects by using the visual arts, dance, drama, and music. As they begin to recognize how different artistic modes, materials, and techniques lead to different responses, they often express strong opinions about the methods and tools they want to use. Examples of how third graders demonstrate their skills include:

- creating a 2- or 3-D representation of an object, place, or event (for example, constructing a model, painting a mural, or creating an intricate collage);
- using body movements, voice, and props to create a vivid interpretation of a favorite scene from a book;
- using a digital camera to photograph patterns in the environment and transfer them to the computer;
- mixing paints to create many colors to paint a realistic forest scene;
- creating complicated architectural structures using building materials.

Preschool-3

1 Responds to artistic creations or events.

Three year olds begin to appreciate the artistic expressions of other people, although this often requires modeling and encouragement from adults. They may watch other children creating or may attend a short children's theater or musical presentation. They show their emerging appreciation by:

- copying the dance steps of a classmate during creative movement;
- humming or moving to the rhythm of recorded music played during a quiet time;
- listening attentively at a children's concert;
- watching as classmates enact a short story or poem;
- copying the play dough cake a classmate made;
- showing sustained interest in a presentation by a puppeteer or actor.

Preschool-4

1 Responds to artistic creations or events.

Many children express their interest in the arts as observers rather than as producers. With teacher guidance, children can begin to comment on each other's work, asking questions about methods used, showing interest in the feelings being expressed, or noticing details. With teacher support, four year olds can attend to and appreciate children's concerts, dance performances, and theater productions. Examples include:

- listening to music tapes during choice time, indicating appreciation through body language and facial expressions;
- watching classmates as they engage in creative movement activities;
- imitating the voice a classmate used to play Papa Bear;
- exclaiming about the skill a classmate displays in painting, modeling with play dough, or building with Legos;
- closely watching a guest magician or musician who is performing for the class.

Kindergarten

1 Responds to artistic creations or events.

Many children express their interest in the arts as observers rather than as producers. Five year olds are able to appreciate the artistic creations of others, the skill of a dancer, or someone's ability to play a musical instrument. They are excited when a picture or sculpture reminds them of people, objects, or events in their own lives. Some ways that children express this appreciation include:

- listening to music tapes or records during choice time, indicating involvement by body language and facial expression;
- commenting to a friend, "I like how you used so many colors to make your picture look stormy.";
- looking at illustrations in a book and appreciating the skill, humor, or beauty of the drawings;
- identifying the painting they liked best in the art museum and telling why;
- listening with attention and pleasure to a visiting artist, such as a poet, writer, musician, or magician;
- drawing pictures of their favorite character in a play;
- watching as classmates put on a puppet show or perform a dance the class created.

First Grade

1 Responds to artistic creations and events.

Many children express their interest in the arts as observers rather than as producers. With encouragement, first graders can begin to appreciate the art of others, whether it is created by their peers, artists, or performers who visit the school, or whether they encounter the work in books, videos, or professional performances. They can describe their preferences and consider some ways the artist has used different techniques to convey a mood, story, or point of view. Some ways first graders respond to artistic creations and events include:

- listening with pleasure to records, tapes, and live musical performances;
- describing artistic elements in patterns in nature (for example, repeating lines, colors, or textures);
- recognizing that an illustration uses colors to convey ideas and emotions;
- hearing music and relating it to real sounds (of animals, cars, machines);
- noticing that an actor's movements can convey ideas and emotions (such as age, anger, or happiness).

Second Grade

1 Interprets and extracts meaning from artistic products and experiences.

Opportunities to use and observe various art forms enable children to think about the artist's purpose and how form and structure are used to convey meaning. Second graders can explore different features of a particular art form (for example, line, color, texture in the visual arts or tempo and lyrics in music). They also develop preferences for particular artistic styles and, with encouragement, can explain their likes and dislikes. Examples include:

- listening with pleasure to records, tapes, and live musical performances and describing personal preferences;
- being attentive during classroom presentations (sharing skits, art work, and other creations);
- recognizing that an illustrator used color, line, and shape to convey ideas and emotions;
- hearing music and relating it to real sounds (of animals, cars, or machines);
- describing how an actor's movements convey specific ideas and emotions (such as joy or rage);
- writing a simple critique of an arts event for the classroom newspaper.

Third Grade

1 Interprets and extracts meaning from artistic products and experiences.

When students have opportunities to use and observe various art forms, they can learn to interpret artistic products and experiences. Third graders can observe art forms and notice details, reflect on the artist's perspective, and form and explain their own interpretations. Some ways students demonstrate their interpretation of the arts include:

- recognizing that an illustrator used color, line, and shape to convey specific ideas and emotions;
- hearing music and reflecting on how the composer created the effects of real sounds (of animals, cars, machines);
- describing how an actor's movements and vocal expression convey specific effects and trying to emulate them;
- representing an artistic experience using a different medium (for example, painting a picture that represents feelings expressed in music);
- writing a "critique" of a music or drama performance for the school newspaper.

B   Understanding and appreciation

Preschool-3

Not expected at this level.

Preschool-4

Not expected at this level.

Kindergarten

Not expected at this level.

First Grade

2 **Begins to recognize cultural and historical connections with the arts.**

As children study their own culture and the culture of others in the present and past, they can explore how culture is expressed through art. First graders can look at paintings and artifacts of their families and communities and learn songs and dances from their own culture and other cultures. Some ways they demonstrate their beginning understanding include:

- listening to or singing songs from the culture of their own family and the families of their classmates;
- looking at art forms in the community (for example, architecture, sculpture, murals) and thinking about when these might have been built or created;
- learning a dance from their own or another culture;
- discussing how music is used for celebrations in different families and cultures;
- learning about songs and dances used in earlier historical times;
- comparing paintings or sculptures from different cultures.

Second Grade

2 **Recognizes cultural and historical connections with the arts.**

As children study their own culture and the culture of others in the past and present, they can explore ways that culture is expressed through art. Second graders can begin to observe and describe similarities and differences in the art, music, and dance of their own and other cultures. Some ways they demonstrate their understanding of cultural and historical connections include:

- studying the illustrations in a picture book by Ezra Jack Keats and describing how the watercolors create the mood of the people in the city;
- listening to a CD of classical music by a famous composer;
- learning the words to folk songs from the past;
- looking at photographs of how their city looked long ago and comparing the architecture of the old buildings to present day architecture.

Third Grade

2 **Demonstrates understanding of how the arts connect with culture and history.**

Third graders are learning to use artifacts and art forms to understand history and culture. They can begin to recognize how people throughout history have used the arts in different ways (for example, to celebrate, depict myths, express religious beliefs). Eight year olds can plan and create detailed artwork, music, and dramatizations depicting scenes from history or reflecting their study of a culture. Some ways they demonstrate their understanding include:

- watching a video of a dance from a different culture and discussing the story the dance is representing;
- listening to the lyrics of a song and reflecting on its historical meaning to the people who originally sang it;
- describing how contemporary music has been influenced by music from different cultures;
- researching a famous artist and attempting to emulate that person's style.

VI The Arts

165

VII

Physical Development and Health

The emphasis in this domain is on physical development as an integral part of children's well-being and educational growth. The components address gross motor skills, fine motor skills, and personal health and safety. A principal focus in gross motor is on children's ability to move in ways that demonstrate control, balance, and coordination. Fine motor skills are equally important in laying the groundwork for artistic expression, handwriting, and self-care skills. The third component addresses children's growing ability to understand and manage their personal health and safety.

VII Physical Development and Health
A Gross motor development

Preschool-3

1 Moves with some balance and control.

Three year olds are very focused on practicing their newly acquired physical skills. They can jump with two feet, hop a few times on each foot, and climb stairs. Running is a joy, as are galloping, dancing, and jumping. Examples of increasing body control include:

- moving around the classroom without bumping into furniture;
- starting, turning, and stopping when running without crashing into things;
- jumping like a frog with both feet together several times in a row;
- using alternating feet when going up stairs (coming down stairs may still be one step at a time without alternating feet);
- walking on a line on the floor;
- galloping with relative ease;
- crawling through a play tunnel or under tables;
- jumping from a large block and landing securely.

Preschool-4

1 Moves with balance and control.

Four year olds are actively refining their gross motor control. They enjoy practicing skills and challenge themselves to jump farther or run faster than their friends. They can run more smoothly than at younger ages, hop on each foot several times, and climb up and down stairs using a more adult-like form. Four year olds show their emerging skills by:

- maintaining balance on a 2 x 4 balance beam that is close to the ground;
- moving around the classroom on narrow paths between furniture without bumping into things;
- developing mastery over running skills (such as quick stops, full circle turns, short 180 degree turns, speeding up and slowing down);
- going up and down stairs alternating feet without holding onto the rail or the wall;
- hopping several times on each foot;
- galloping with a smooth gait and relative ease.

Kindergarten

1 Moves with balance and control.

Five year olds are very active, seeming to be in constant motion. For the most part, their movements are under control even though they now move more quickly and with greater agility than in the past. Kindergarten children can run smoothly, hop many times on each foot, and climb up and down stairs using alternating feet. Some ways that children show their growing balance and control include:

- moving through an obstacle course forwards and sideways using a variety of movements with ease;
- stopping and starting movements in response to a signal;
- maintaining balance while bending, twisting, or stretching;
- walking up or down stairs while holding an object in one or both hands;
- carrying a glass of water or juice across the room without spilling it;
- moving confidently around the room, in the halls, and when going up and down stairs.

First Grade

1 Moves with balance and control.

Six year olds are very active and work hard to master a variety of gross motor tasks that require balance and control. Because they are growing quickly, their efforts to control their bodies are not always successful. Examples of how they demonstrate increasing skills include:

- walking across the cafeteria carrying a lunch tray without mishap;
- reaching for materials on a high shelf and successfully getting what they need;
- distributing materials (books, papers, art materials) in the classroom without dropping them;
- playing on outdoor equipment with ease (such as climbers and swings);
- running on the playground, yet carefully dodging objects or other people.

Second Grade

1 Moves with agility, balance, and control.

As seven year olds develop more balance and control, they can move with greater speed, accuracy, and agility in many different activities. Examples of how they demonstrate increasing balance and control include:

- walking with fluid, sure steps, and moving easily through the classroom and hallways;
- distributing materials (books, papers, art materials) in the classroom without dropping them;
- running easily on the playground or in the gym and being able to swerve, dodge, and change directions suddenly;
- running around the bases during a kickball game;
- carrying a large box of supplies and maneuvering to get it into the closet.

Third Grade

1 Moves with agility, speed, and control while performing gross motor tasks.

Because the energy level of eight year olds is high, they move around a great deal. Moving with greater speed, accuracy, and agility in many different activities is typical of third graders. Some ways they demonstrate this development include:

- moving furniture easily in the classroom in order to make room for special activities (a skit, game, or movement activity);
- running easily with the ability to swerve, dodge, and change directions suddenly in tag games;
- learning a series of jump rope tricks and combining them into a routine;
- running in relay races.

VII Physical Development and Health

A Gross motor development

Preschool-3

2 Coordinates movements to perform simple tasks.

As three year olds learn to control their bodies, they are able to combine several independent skills to perform more advanced movements. For example, throwing a ball requires not only a thrusting motion, but also the ability to release the ball at the proper moment to send it in the right direction. Three year olds show this growing coordination by:

- catching a large ball with two hands;
- throwing a ball into a basket;
- kicking a large stationary ball in a forward direction;
- climbing the ladder of the slide, holding onto the rail while moving each foot up a step;
- pedaling and steering a tricycle around the playground or gym without crashing;
- climbing onto the swing seat unassisted;
- scrambling up the side of a low jungle gym;
- throwing a bean bag to another person so that it can be caught.

Preschool-4

2 Coordinates movements to perform simple tasks.

Four year olds are able to combine movements to accomplish increasingly challenging physical tasks. They can now kick balls, aim and throw bean bags, climb and swing on jungle gyms, and ride tricycles with increasing control. They love to practice these new skills in games, especially with adult companions. Ways they show increasing coordination include:

- throwing a ball in the right direction, aiming at a target with reasonable accuracy;
- catching a ball by moving their arms or bodies to adjust for the direction the ball is traveling;
- kicking a large ball with a two-step start;
- riding a tricycle on a path around the playground;
- using the slide, seesaw, or swings;
- hitting a stationary target with an overhand throw.

Kindergarten

2 Coordinates movements to perform tasks.

Five year olds are busy experimenting with how their bodies move. They are ready to combine various independent skills to accomplish new feats and meet new challenges. These include:

- moving their bodies into position to catch a ball, then throwing the ball in the right direction;
- bouncing a ball and catching it;
- kicking a stationary ball using a smooth running step;
- sweeping with a broom and using a dust pan;
- skipping smoothly, alternating feet;
- hanging a picture on a wall with tape or push pins;
- throwing a medium-sized ball with some accuracy;
- walking, galloping, jumping, and running in rhythm to simple tunes and music patterns.

First Grade

2 Coordinates movements to perform tasks.

Most six year olds are developing the ability to move with coordination in planned and skillful ways that combine several kinds of movements simultaneously. Examples include:

- jumping and turning a rope at the same time;
- performing a simple dance that involves moving and clapping;
- moving to music in a coordinated way;
- throwing and catching a ball;
- running and then kicking a soccer ball.

Second Grade

2 Coordinates movements to perform tasks.

Most seven year olds can move with coordination in planned and skillful ways that involve several kinds of simultaneous movements. Examples include:

- combining several moves while jumping rope;
- completing a series of tumbling acts (such as somersaults and cartwheels);
- playing ball games that require coordination (tether ball, four-square, kickball);
- performing simple dance steps while using rhythm instruments.

Third Grade

2 Demonstrates coordinated movements in games, sports, and other activities.

By third grade, students are very coordinated and can integrate their physical skills into sports, gymnastics, and dance. Examples include:

- performing a series of tumbling maneuvers (such as cartwheels and flips);
- running and then kicking a soccer ball during a game;
- swinging a bat and hitting a ball;
- performing intricate dance steps;
- throwing and catching a ball in skillful ways (in a softball game, while playing dodgeball, and so forth).

Preschool-3

1 Uses strength and control to perform simple tasks.

Three year olds are just beginning to develop enough fine motor ability to perform many simple tasks. They are very interested in trying to use new materials and tools that are available in the classroom. They will engage in the same task over and over again, gaining mastery and strength as they work. They show persistence in gaining fine motor control by:

- pushing marker caps off and on;
- pushing Pop-It beads together and then pulling them apart;
- tearing a piece of tape off the tape dispenser (but often getting the tape stuck together in the process);
- putting Duplos, Legos, or Bristle Blocks together and taking them apart;
- experimenting with the use of scissors;
- placing pegs into the peg board and then removing them to see how they fit and whether all the holes can be filled.

Preschool-4

1 Uses strength and control to perform simple tasks.

Four year olds continue to develop fine motor skills through their participation in classroom activities. By using many different classroom materials (such as art materials and tools, manipulatives, and the workbench), they improve their hand and finger strength and control. Examples of their efforts include:

- using clothespins to hang paintings or pretend laundry;
- putting Bristle Blocks or Pop-It beads together and pulling them apart;
- pushing a cookie cutter into dough;
- pulling the caps off markers and putting them back on firmly;
- using the paper punch to make holes;
- twisting the cap off a jar of paste;
- cutting off tape with scissors or using the tape dispenser's serrated edge;
- pulling apart Lego blocks with relative ease.

Kindergarten

1 Uses strength and control to accomplish tasks.

Five year olds are becoming adept at using the small muscles of their hands and fingers to accomplish more difficult tasks. Over time, their hand strength and control improves. Since some children are more skillful than others, it is important to look for growth rather than specific accomplishments at this age of transition. Examples of growing strength and control include:

- using a stapler to join several pages;
- using a paper punch without help;
- making complex forms and designs stretching rubber bands across geoboards;
- removing and replacing lids and caps of containers;
- hammering two pieces of wood together to make an airplane;
- tearing a piece of tape off a roll of tape without letting the tape get stuck to itself.

First Grade

1 Uses strength, control, and eye-hand coordination to accomplish tasks.

As first graders develop more strength and control in their hands and wrists, they become increasingly able to use materials with intent and precision. The increasing eye-hand coordination of six year olds enables them to complete fine motor tasks when only one type of movement is involved. Combining several movements sometimes leads to frustration. Some ways they demonstrate improving coordination are:

- using scissors to cut out an outlined figure;
- placing blocks on a structure without knocking it down;
- tearing paper into specific shapes to make a collage;
- using a stapler to join several pages of a story;
- sewing clothing on a puppet;
- fitting pattern blocks and tangrams into pre-drawn outlines;
- striking the keys of a calculator, computer game, or keyboard with increasing accuracy.

Second Grade

1 Uses strength, control, and eye-hand coordination to accomplish tasks.

By seven, children have strength and dexterity in their fingers, hands, and wrists. Their increasing eye-hand coordination is demonstrated by their ability to write small letters and include fine details in their drawings. They can combine several of these skills in an organized way to produce a product. Some examples include:

- using a stapler or hole punch effectively;
- using scissors to cut straight and curved lines and shapes;
- working with woodworking tools;
- attaching pieces of cardboard together with masking tape or brads to create a 3-D object;
- using a compass to draw a circle;
- using a computer keyboard and mouse with increasing accuracy.

Third Grade

1 Uses strength, control, and eye-hand coordination to accomplish tasks.

Eight year olds have increased dexterity and eye-hand coordination, enabling them to perform a variety of fine motor tasks in an organized way. Examples of this include:

- using woodworking tools to complete a project;
- playing a computer game that requires speed and accuracy;
- creating a beadwork pattern using a needle, string, and beads;
- using tweezers to prepare a microscope slide (for example, placing a fish scale or insect part on a slide);
- threading a needle.

Preschool-3

2   Uses eye-hand coordination to perform simple tasks.

Developing eye-hand coordination is challenging for three year olds. Although they are just beginning to learn how to manipulate scissors, they can build with blocks, complete simple puzzles, and string beads. They learn to combine their fine motor and perceptual abilities when they play and work with manipulatives in the classroom. Examples include:

- turning a puzzle piece several different ways to find the right fit;
- building a tall tower, eight to ten blocks high;
- rejecting puzzle pieces that don't fit, rather than trying to pound them in;
- making patterns in the sand with their fingers and tracks with toy cars;
- experimenting with making "bridges" and "houses," and other real-life structures out of one-inch cubes.

Preschool-4

2   Uses eye-hand coordination to perform tasks.

Four year olds demonstrate their eye-hand coordination skills as they start to construct with unit blocks, Tinker Toys, and Legos; put together puzzles; and experiment at the sand and water tables. Their artwork tends to become more complicated as they use newly mastered skills to create products. Examples of eye-hand coordination include:

- zipping coats;
- cutting on a line or around a large picture with scissors;
- stringing beads or pasta with holes onto a length of yarn;
- dressing dolls using snaps and buttons;
- constructing or copying buildings and roads with the table blocks;
- explaining to a classmate how to place individual puzzle pieces by matching shapes or colors or looking at picture clues;
- using a hammer to try to pound nails into soft wood.

Kindergarten

2   Uses eye-hand coordination to perform tasks effectively.

Five year olds are continuing to improve their eye-hand coordination and accomplishing tasks with greater precision. They enjoy playing with manipulatives and blocks and sometimes work with a finished product in mind. Five year olds demonstrate eye-hand coordination by:

- putting together 18- to 25-piece puzzles using picture as well as shape clues;
- dressing in a variety of costumes in the dramatic play area (buttoning shirts, zipping jackets);
- building specific block structures from a model without knocking the structures down;
- cutting fabric into shapes to use for collage;
- using tape, stapler, and glue to create 3-D objects, such as a house or an airplane;
- constructing planned projects out of Legos, Bristle Blocks, table blocks, and Tinker Toys.

First Grade

See the following indicator on page 173 in Physical Development and Health:

B Fine motor development

1 Uses strength, control, and eye-hand coordination to accomplish tasks.

Second Grade

See the following indicator on page 173 in Physical Development and Health:

B Fine motor development

1 Uses strength, control, and eye-hand coordination to accomplish tasks.

Third Grade

See the following indicator on page 173 in Physical Development and Health:

B Fine motor development

1 Uses strength, control, and eye-hand coordination to accomplish tasks.

Preschool-3

3 Explores the use of various drawing and art tools.

This is the age when children first experiment with drawing implements and other art tools. As a result of these explorations, they develop the control from which writing skills eventually emerge. They use many different grasps, both hands, and even whole arms as they practice. Examples of experimentation include:

- using different drawing tools, such as crayons, markers, and chalk;
- experimenting with sponges, brushes, Q-tips, and other tools for painting lines and shapes;
- painting at the easel, trying big and small brushes and different strokes, all the while watching the effect of their hand and arm movements;
- sprinkling glitter on lines of glue or pasting many felt shapes on top of each other;
- swirling finger paint around and noticing the way patterns appear and disappear.

Preschool-4

3 Shows beginning control of writing, drawing, and art tools.

Four year olds are interested in the process of drawing and writing. However, the finished product is not as important to them as the process of creation. At this age, children begin to use a more conventional grasp, and even practice making some letters for their names or for signs. Four year olds show their growing control over writing and drawing tools by:

- drawing with markers and then deciding that the picture is a dog, a monster, or "me";
- using chalk on the blackboard, pretending to write letters or numbers;
- holding a pencil in a pincer grasp;
- using glue sticks to paste a variety of items on their collages;
- trying a variety of ways to make brush strokes at the easel.

Kindergarten

3 Uses writing and drawing tools with some control.

At five, children's increased strength and coordination allow them to use a variety of writing, drawing, and art tools with greater control. As their pencil grasp becomes established, some show interest in the rudimentary formation of letters and repeatedly practice writing their names and other words. At this age, children demonstrate their control of writing tools by:

- drawing pictures, designs, and letters with pencils, pens, crayons, or markers;
- holding a pencil in a mature grasp rather than with their fists;
- writing their first names legibly without help;
- using a pencil with their preferred hand while holding the paper in position with the other hand;
- using scissors to cut simple shapes and pictures, only occasionally straying off the line;
- painting with different sized brushes to create shapes, designs and figures;
- using pencils, pens, and paints and brushes to form letters and symbols or to make repeating patterns.

First Grade

2 Uses writing and drawing tools with some control.

Most first graders use pencils, crayons, and markers with increasing frequency and control. Because they realize the results are not always perfect, they may show some lack of confidence in their drawing and writing abilities. Some ways that six year olds show they are developing necessary handwriting skills are:

- holding pencils, crayons, and markers with a comfortable grip;
- forming letters and numbers so they are legible;
- using one hand to write and the other to hold the paper;
- writing a note that is neat;
- controlling pens that have different kinds of points;
- using a straight-edge or ruler with one hand and drawing a line along it with the other.

Second Grade

2 Uses writing and drawing tools with some confidence and control.

By seven, children can form letters and numbers with relative ease and can control the placement of letters on a page. Their drawings are smaller and more detailed. Some ways that seven year olds show increasing handwriting and drawing skills are:

- using crayons, markers, and paint brushes to create detailed representational images;
- forming upper- and lowercase letters with accuracy and neatness;
- creating "fancy letters" to put on the cover of a story they wrote or on their portfolios;
- beginning to develop a handwriting style (such as forming certain letters in a particular way).

Third Grade

2 Uses writing tools with confidence and control.

Third graders have good control of handwriting and can learn to use cursive writing. Their often-sloppy, informal handwriting is frequently the result of their tendency to rush. When they take the time to write slowly, their handwriting can be clear and legible. Examples include:

- using writing tools with increasing ease for a purpose (such as writing stories, lists, letters, and charts);
- writing legibly with good spacing;
- beginning to use cursive writing;
- using various art media with confidence and control.

Preschool-3

1 **Begins to perform self-care tasks independently.**

Three year olds are just learning how to manage their personal care on their own. They still need adult support and guidance, but they are eager to try to do things for themselves. This is the age when they can become very involved in cleanliness and order. Self-help skills include:

- putting on some of their own outside clothes;
- pouring from a small pitcher into a glass;
- attaching velcro closures on sneakers;
- spreading peanut butter with a knife;
- buttoning and unbuttoning large buttons;
- pulling up their pants after using the toilet;
- washing their hands and drying them, with verbal prompts and support.

Preschool-4

1 **Performs some self-care tasks independently.**

Four year olds love performing self-care tasks and daily routines on their own. Sometimes they need guidance to avoid becoming silly or to remember what they are doing. They forget rules easily because they are busy with other thoughts, but they can usually meet expectations after verbal reminders. They show growing self-care skills by:

- using the toilet independently;
- washing and drying hands with only occasional reminders;
- managing dressing tasks independently (such as putting on coats, pants, and boots);
- pouring juice or milk from a small pitcher without spilling;
- mastering zippers, buttons and some buckles (tying shoes is not yet expected);
- using tissues to wipe their noses and throwing the tissues in the wastebasket.

Kindergarten

1 **Performs self-care tasks competently.**

Kindergartners are quite competent about taking care of their own physical needs and often volunteer to help classmates who are struggling with buttons and laces. They take pride in their skills and will often practice zipping jackets and tying bows just for the pleasure of doing it. They demonstrate competence by:

- taking care of their own toilet needs, asking for help with suspenders or other complicated clothing;
- remembering to wash their hands before snack;
- putting on their own outdoor clothing with very little help and few reminders;
- pouring juice easily and without spills for snack or lunch;
- spreading peanut butter and doing other simple tasks with food;
- keeping track of their personal belongings and taking responsibility for keeping them safe;
- cleaning up art projects or other messy activities with relative skill.

First Grade

1 **Practices basic strategies for personal health and safety.**

First graders are gaining competence and independence in performing self-care tasks and recognizing that their behavior affects their health and safety. Some strategies they use to practice personal health and safety are:

- using tissues without a reminder to wipe runny noses;
- dressing independently and appropriately for the weather (knowing to wear mittens, gloves, hats, or scarves when it is cold outside);
- washing hands before snack or lunch times and after using the bathroom;
- seeking help from a familiar adult when a parent does not show up after school, rather than standing alone in front of the school building.

Second Grade

1 **Practices basic strategies for personal health and safety.**

Second graders can apply basic hygiene habits regularly and independently (for example, brushing teeth, washing hands). They know what to do in an emergency and how to seek assistance in a difficult situation. Some strategies they use are:

- washing hands before lunch and after going to the bathroom;
- covering their noses or mouths when sneezing and coughing;
- knowing and obeying fire drill rules;
- identifying people who can help in emergency situations;
- wearing a seatbelt on the bus;
- following traffic safety rules such as crossing at corners, looking both ways, not running into the street to get a ball.

Third Grade

1 **Begins to problem-solve and make decisions that promote personal health and safety.**

By third grade, students understand what is needed to keep the body healthy and safe: nutritious food, adequate rest, and personal hygiene. They recognize how their actions can affect their well-being. Some examples of ways they promote personal health and safety include:

- using actions that help prevent germs from spreading (such as covering their noses or mouths when coughing and sneezing, and washing and drying hands before handling food);
- identifying behaviors to use in emergency situations (for example, knowing and obeying fire drill rules);
- participating regularly in fitness activities;
- explaining to a classmate reasons for wearing helmets when riding bicycles;
- participating in a class discussion about different ways to handle family stress;
- maintaining good personal hygiene (for example, keeping their bodies and hair clean and neat).

Preschool-3

2 Follows basic health and safety rules with reminders.

Three year olds are beginning to learn rules for health and safety. Washing hands after using the toilet, covering their mouths when they sneeze or cough, and staying inside the yard are all rules that they can remember; however, they may not fully understand the reasons for these rules. Children this age show they are learning basic rules by:

- washing their hands before snack or the cooking project (after being reminded);
- avoiding the area in front of the swings on the playground when children are swinging;
- knowing some common safety rules that have been discussed (for example, always waiting on the sidewalk until the bus aide comes to take them to the bus);
- avoiding dangers such as hot stoves and sharp knives;
- leaving the room only when given permission to do so;
- holding someone's hand whenever walking outside the school grounds.

Preschool-4

2 Follows basic health and safety rules.

Four year olds are becoming aware of some health and safety issues. They can begin to learn about their need for food, water, and shelter, and how to keep themselves safe. They enjoy stories about their bodies and other health issues and will discuss these issues with their friends. They show their beginning understanding of health and safety rules by:

- trying different foods that are introduced by the teacher as nutritious, and discussing with classmates what "nutritious" means;
- acting out fire safety procedures (stop, drop, and roll);
- carrying scissors and pencils with points down to avoid accidents;
- washing their hands after using the toilet or before snack and lunch;
- standing far enough away from swings in use to avoid injury;
- discussing the roles of dentists, doctors, and nurses in keeping people healthy;
- covering their mouths when coughing.

Kindergarten

2 Shows beginning understanding of and follows health and safety rules.

Five year olds are interested in health and safety issues, especially when these relate to their own experiences. Although they still need reminders to follow health and safety rules, they are beginning to understand the rationale for these rules. Examples include:

- telling a friend not to run in front of the school bus or a car;
- remembering to put on their seat belts when going home on the bus;
- discussing what dentists and doctors do to keep people healthy;
- talking about which foods they eat during snack or lunch times and whether these are nutritious;
- discussing safety rules when on a class trip, such as waiting behind a leader before crossing a street;
- understanding why fire drills are important;
- discussing traffic safety rules as they engage in dramatic play or build roads and cities out of blocks.

First Grade

2 **Demonstrates some beginning awareness of issues related to health and safety.**

First graders are learning how to stay healthy and safe through personal hygiene, nutritious food at regular intervals, and adequate rest. They can identify people and places in the community who can help with health issues (clinics, doctors, nurses, dentists) and safety issues (firefighters, police). Some examples of their growing understanding of personal health and safety are:

- identifying people who can help in emergency situations;
- talking about healthy snack choices to a friend at lunch;
- describing the importance of brushing teeth and visiting the dentist regularly;
- knowing not to talk to strangers on the street;
- knowing the phone number to call in case of fire or other emergency;
- describing ways to prevent common illnesses (for example, that covering the mouth or nose when sneezing or coughing prevents cold germs from spreading).

Second Grade

2 **Demonstrates beginning awareness of current issues related to health and safety.**

Second grade children are learning about health and safety issues. They have some basic knowledge of nutrition, how the body develops, common illnesses, and basic ways to prevent common illnesses. Examples of second graders' growing awareness of health and safety issues include:

- describing safety practices on the playground;
- creating a chart of a healthy diet and listing foods in each of the basic food groups;
- retelling a news story related to health;
- participating in a class discussion about the differences between helpful and harmful substances;
- listening with interest to a presentation on fire prevention.

Third Grade

2 **Demonstrates some awareness of current issues related to health and safety.**

Third graders are gaining increased understanding of the importance of maintaining good health and abiding by safety rules. Although many health and safety issues are beyond their control, they ask questions and seek out information about environmental factors that affect health and safety, illness and disease prevention, and substance use and abuse. Examples of their growing awareness of health and safety issues include:

- presenting a report on practices that might be dangerous to health (such as smoking, drinking, and using drugs);
- asking questions during an assembly presentation about environmental health hazards;
- writing a research report describing one of the systems of the human body;
- comparing labels on food products to determine fat and sugar content and the presence of preservatives;
- creating a chart summarizing common illnesses and methods of prevention.

VII Physical Development and Health

References

Achieve [Resource Center for Governors and Business Leaders on Academic Standards, Assessment, Accountability, and Technology]. (1986). *Standards initiatives*. Cambridge, MA; Washington, DC: Author. Retrieved from : http://www.achieve.org

Adams, M. J. (1990). *Beginning to read: Thinking and learning about print*. Cambridge, MA: The MIT Press.

Adams, M. J., Foorman, B. R., Lundberg, I., & Beeler, T. (1998). *Phonemic awareness in young children: A classroom curriculum*. Baltimore, MD: Paul H. Brookes Publishing Co.

Althouse, R., & Main, C. (1975). *Science experiences for young children*. New York, NY: Teachers College Press.

American Association for the Advancement of Science. (1993). *Benchmarks for science literacy*. New York, NY: Oxford University Press.

American Association for the Advancement of Science. (1998). *Dialogue on early childhood science, mathematics, and technology education*. Forum on early childhood science, mathematics, and technology education. New York, NY: Author.

American Association for the Advancement of Science. (1990). *Science for all Americans*. New York, NY: Oxford University Press.

American Historical Association. (1996). *National standards for history: UCLA national standards for history grades K-4: Expanding children's world in time and space*. Los Angeles, CA: Author. Retrieved from http://www.theaha.org/k12/

Arizona Department of Education Academic Standards and Accountability Division. (2000). *Academic standards and aims: Language arts, math, science, social studies*. Phoenix, AZ: Author. Retrieved from http://www.ade.state.as.us/standards

Armington, D. (1997). *The living classroom: Writing, reading, and beyond*. Washington, DC: National Association for the Education of Young Children.

Bank Street College of Education & The Northwest Regional Educational Laboratory. (2000). *LEARNS literacy assessment profile*. New York, NY: Author.

Bodrova, E., Leong, D. J., Paynter, D. E., & Semenov, D. (2000). *A framework for early literacy instruction: Aligning standards to developmental accomplishments and student behaviors: Pre-K through kindergarten*. Aurora, CO: Mid-continent Regional Educational Laboratory, Inc.

Boston Public Schools. (1996). *Citywide learning standards and curriculum framework*. Boston, MA: Author. Retrieved from http://www.boston.k12.ma.us/teach/standards.

Bredekamp, S., & Rosegrant, T. (Eds.). (1995). *Reaching potentials: Transforming early childhood curriculum and assessment* (Vol. 2). Washington, DC: National Association for the Education of Young Children.

Burke, M. J., & Curcio, F. R. (2000). *Learning mathematics for a new century: NCTM 2000 Yearbook*. Reston, VA: National Council of Teachers of Mathematics.

Burns, M. (1992). *About teaching mathematics: A K-8 resource*. White Plains, NY: Cuisenaire Company of America.

Burns, M. S., Griffin, P., & Snow, C. E. (Eds.). (1999). *Starting out right: A guide to promoting children's reading success*. Washington, DC: National Academy Press.

California State Board of Education Standards and Assessment Division. (1999). *Academic content standards for California public schools: English language development, mathematics, history-social science, science, visual and performing arts*. Sacramento, CA: Author. Retrieved from: http://www.cde.ca.gov/board

Campbell, R. (Ed.). (1998). *Facilitating preschool literacy*. Newark, DE: International Reading Association.

Clay, M. M. (1993). *An observation survey of early literacy achievement*. Auckland, New Zealand: Heinemann.

Clay, M. M. (1985). *The early detection of reading difficulties*. Auckland, New Zealand: Heinemann.

Clements, D. H. (1999). Geometry and spatial thinking in young children. In J. V. Copley, (Ed.). *Mathematics in the early years* (pp. 66-79). Reston, VA: NCTM; Washington, DC: National Association for the Education of Young Children.

Committee on Science Education K-12. (1998). *Every child a scientist: Achieving scientific literacy for all*. Washington, DC: National Academy Press.

Connecticut State Department of Education. (1999). *Preschool curriculum framework and benchmarks for children in preschool programs*. Hartford, CT: Author. Retrieved from: http//www.state.ct.us/sed/dtl/curriculum/

Connecticut State Department of Education Division of Teaching and Learning. (1998). *Common Core of Learning: Social studies*. Hartford, CT: Author. Retrieved from http://www.state.ct.us/sed/dtl/curriculum/

Copley, J. V. (Ed.). (2000). *Mathematics in the early years*. Reston, VA: NCTM; Washington, DC: National Association for the Education of Young Children.

Copley, J. V. (2000). *The young child and mathematics*. Washington, DC: National Association for the Education of Young Children.

Darp. P., Hampton, S., & Resnick, L. B. (1999). *New Standards: Primary literacy standards for kindergarten through third grade.* Washington, DC: National Center on Education & the Economy and the University of Pittsburgh.

Department of Defense Education Activity (DODEA). (2000). *Elementary (K-6) Curriculum Standards: Language arts.* Arlington, VA: Author. Retrieved from: http://www.odedodea.edu/curriculum

De Villiers, P. A., & De Villiers, J. G. (1979). *Early language.* Cambridge, MA: Harvard University Press.

Donahue, P. L., Voelkl, K. E., Campbell, J. R., & Mazzeo, J. (1999). *The NAEP reading report card for the nation and the states, NCES 1999.* Washington, DC: U.S. Department of Education, Office of Educational Research and Improvement, National Center for Education Statistics.

Florida Department of Education, Curriculum, Instruction and Assessment. (1996). *Sunshine state standards: English/language arts, math, science, social studies.* Tallahassee, FL: Author. Retrieved from: http://www.firn.edu/doe/menu/sss.htm

Fountas, I. C., & Pinnell, G. S. (1998). *Word matters: Teaching phonics and spelling in the reading/writing classroom.* Portsmouth, NH: Heinemann.

Garton, A. & Pratt, C. (1998). *Learning to be literate: The development of spoken and written language.* Malden, MA: Blackwell Publishers, Inc.

Harlan, J.D. (1976). *Science experiences for the early childhood years.* Columbus, OH: Charles E. Merrill Publishing Company.

Harlen, W. (1989). *Developing science in the primary classroom.* Portsmouth, NH: Heinemann.

Holt, B. G. (1989). *Science with young children.* Washington, DC: National Association for the Education of Young Children.

Haylock, D., & Cockburn, A. (1997). *Understanding mathematics in the lower primary years (revised and expanded edition).* London, England: Paul Chapman Publishing LTD.

Idaho State Board of Education. (2000). *Idaho's standards for excellence: Science.* Boise, ID: Author. Retrieved from: http://www.sde.state.id.us/osbe/exstand.htm

International Reading Association & National Association for the Education of Young Children. (1998). *Learning to read and write: Developmentally appropriate practices for young children.* Joint Position Statement. Washington, DC: National Association for the Education of Young Children.

International Reading Association & National Council of Teachers of English. (1996). *Standards for the English language arts.* Newark, DE; Washington, DC: Author.

Kendall, J. S., & Marzano, R. J. (1997). *Content knowledge: A compendium of standards and benchmarks for K-12 education.* (2nd ed.). Alexandria, VA: Association for Supervision and Curriculum Development. Aurora, CO: Mid-continent Regional Educational Laboratory, Inc.

Kentucky Department of Education Division of Curriculum Development (1999). *Core content for assessment: Language arts.* Frankfort, KY: Author. Retrieved from: http://www.kde.state.ky.us/oapd/curric/corecontent/

Machado, J. M. (1999). *Early childhood experience in language arts: Emerging literacy.* (6th ed.). Albany, New York: Delmar Publishers.

Maryland Department of Education. (2000). *Maryland state content standards: Language arts, math, social studies.* Annapolis, MD: Author. Retrieved from: http://www.mdk12.org/mspp/standards

Meisels, S. J., Atkins-Burnett, S., & Nicholson, J. (1996). *Assessment of social competence, adaptive behaviors, and approaches to learning.* Working Paper #96-18, National Center for Education Statistics. Washington, DC: U.S. Department of Education, Office of Educational Research and Improvement.

Michigan State Board of Education Early Childhood Education, Parenting and Comprehensive School Health Unit. (1992). *Early childhood standards of quality: For prekindergarten through second grade.* Lansing, MI: Author.

Minnesota Department of Children, Families and Learning. (1998). *The Minnesota graduation standards, profile of learning, content standards: Language arts, math, social studies.* St. Paul, MN: Author.

Montgomery County Public Schools. (2000). *Maryland State Content Standards.* Annapolis, MD: Maryland Department of Education. Retrieved from: http://www.mcps.k12.md.us/departments

Morrow, L. M. (1997). *Literacy development in the early years: Helping children read and write.* (3rd ed.). Boston: Allyn and Bacon.

National Association for the Education of Young Children. (1998). General NAEYC accreditation information. Washington DC: Author. Retrieved from: http://www.naeyc.org/accreditation

National Association for Sport and Physical Education. (1995). *Moving into the future: National physical education standards: A guide to content and assessment.* Reston, VA: Author.

National Center on Education and the Economy & The Learning Research and Development Center, University of Pittsburgh. (1999). *Reading and writing grade by grade: Primary literacy standards for kindergarten through third grade.* Washington, DC: Author.

National Center for History in the Schools. (1996). *National standards for history, basic education.* Los Angeles, CA: Author. Retrieved from: http://www.sscnet.ucla.edu/nchs/standards/

National Council for the Social Studies. (1994). *Curriculum standards for social studies.* Washington, DC: Author.

National Council of Teachers of Mathematics. (2000). *Principles and standards for school mathematics.* Reston, VA: Author. Retrieved from: http://standards.nctm.org

National Education Goals Panel. (1997). *Reconsidering children's early development and learning: Toward common views and vocabulary.* Washington, DC: Author.

National Research Council. (1998). *Every child a scientist: Achieving scientific literacy for all.* Washington, DC: National Academy Press.

National Research Council. (1996). *National science education standards.* Washington, DC: National Academy Press. Retrieved from: http://www.nap.edu/readingroom/books/nses/html.

National Standards for Arts Education. (1994). *What every young American should know and be able to do in the arts.* Rowley, MA: Author. Retrieved from: http://didaxinc.com/standards/artstandards.html

Nebraska Department of Education & Iowa Department of Education. (1994). *Primary program: Growing and learning in the heartland.* Lincoln, NB/ DesMoines, IA: Author.

Nebraska State Board of Education. (1998). *Nebraska LEARNS: Reading/writing, social studies/history.* Lincoln, NB: Author. Retrieved from: http://www.edneb.org/IPS/lssu/AcadStand.html

Neuman, S. B., Copple, C., & Bredekamp, S. (2000). *Learning to read and write: Developmentally appropriate practices for young children.* Washington, DC: National Association for the Education of Young Children.

Neuman, S. B. & Roskos, K. A. (Eds.). (1998). *Children achieving: Best practices in early literacy.* Newark, DE: International Reading Association.

New Jersey Department of Education. (2000). *Early childhood education program expectations.* Trenton, NJ: Author. Retrieved from: http//www.state.nj.us/njded/ece/expectations/expectations.htm

New York Department of Education. (1996). *Learning Standards: English language arts.* Albany, NY: Author. Retrieved from: http://www.emsc.nysed.gov/ciai/ela/pub

North Carolina Department of Education. (1999). *Student accountability standards: science, social studies.* Raleigh, NC: Author. Retrieved from : http://www.ncpublicschools.org/curriculum

Oklahoma Department of Education. (2000). *Priority academic student skills: Social studies.* Oklahoma City, OK: Author. Retrieved from : http://www.sde.state.ok.us/publ/pass.html

Oregon Department of Education. (1998). *Oregon academic standards: Social studies.* Salem, OR: Author. Retrieved from : http://www.ode.state.or.us/cifs/standards.htm

Owocki, G. (1999). *Literacy through play.* Portsmouth, NH: Heinemann.

Pinnell, G. S., & Fountas, I. C. (1998). *Word matters: Teaching phonics and spelling in the reading/writing classroom.* Portsmouth, NH: Heinemann.

Putnam Valley Central Schools. (2000). *Developing Educational Standards.* Putnam Valley, NY: Author. Retrieved from : http://www.putnamvlleyschools.org

Raison, G., & Rivalland, J. (1994). *Writing Developmental Continuum.* Portsmouth, NH: Heinemann.

Rees, D., & Rivalland, J. (1997). *Spelling Developmental Continuum.* Portsmouth, NH: Heinemann.

Rees, D., & Shortland-Jones, B. (1994). *Reading Developmental Continuum.* Portsmouth, NH: Heinemann.

Rockwell, R., Hoge, D. R., & Searcy, B. (1999). *Linking language: Simple language and literacy activities throughout the curriculum.* Beltsville, MD: Gryphon House.

Routman, R. (2000). *Conversations: Strategies for teaching, learning, and evaluating.* Portsmouth, NH: Heinemann.

Schickedanz, J. A. (1999). *Much more than the a b c's: The early stages of reading and writing.* Washington, DC: National Association for the Education of Young Children.

Seefeldt, C. (Ed.). *The early childhood curriculum: Current findings in theory and practice.* (3rd ed.). New York: Teachers College Press.

Seefeldt, C. (2001). *Social studies for the preschool/primary child.* Upper Saddle River, NJ: Merrill-Prentice Hall.

Snow, C. E., Burns, M. S., & Griffin, P. (Eds.). (1998). *Preventing reading difficulties in young children.* Washington, DC: National Academy Press.

Soderman, A. K., Gregory, K. M., & O'Neill, L. T. (1999). *Scaffolding emergent literacy: A child-centered approach for preschool through grade 5.* Needham Heights, MA: Allyn & Bacon.

Strickland, D. S. & Morrow, L. M. (Eds.). (1989). *Emerging literacy: Young children learn to read and write.* Newark, DE: International Reading Association.

South Carolina State Department of Education. (1999). *Curriculum standards: Math.* Columbia, SC: Author. Retrieved from : http://www.state.sc.us/sde/educator/crindex.htm

Teachers of English to Speakers of Other Languages, Inc. (1997). *The ESL standards for pre-K-12 students.* Alexandria, VA: Author.

Texas Education Agency. (1997). *Texas essential knowledge and skills: Learning standards for Texas children.* Austin, TX: Author. Retrieved from : http://www.tea.state.tx.ux/teks

U.S. Department of Health and Human Services. (2000). *Head Start Program Performance Standards and Other Regulations (45cfr1301-1311).* Washington, DC: Author.

University of Chicago School Mathematics Project. (1998). *Everyday Mathematics.* Chicago, IL: Everyday Learning.

Virginia Department of Education Division of Instruction. (1999). *Standards of learning for Virginia public schools: Language arts, science, history.* Richmond, VA: Author. Retrieved from : http://www.pen.k12.va.us/

Vermont Department of Education. (2000). *Vermont's framework of standards and learning opportunities: Language arts.* Retrieved from : http://www.State.Vt.us/educ/stand/framework.htm

Wixson, K. K., & Dutro, E. (1998). *Standards for primary grade reading: An analysis of state frameworks.* Ann Arbor, MI: Center for the Improvement of Early Reading Achievement.

Weitzman. E. (1992). *Learning language and loving it.* Toronto, Ont: The Hanen Centre.

Acknowledgements

Fourth Edition:

The authors would like to thank the many individuals who played key roles in helping us complete this revision. The following colleagues provided detailed reviews of drafts of the fourth edition: Linda Borgsdorf (Rebus Inc), Aviva Dorfman (University of Michigan), Debbie Harmon (Eastern Michigan University), Charlotte Stetson (Brattleboro, Vermont), Sue Bredekamp, (Council for Professional Recognition, Washington, D.C.), Susan Neuman (University of Michigan), Doug Clements (SUNY Buffalo), Kathy DeRanna, (California Science Project), Michael Padilla (University of Georgia), Charles Peters (University of Michigan), Michael Yocum (Oakland, MI, Intermediate School District), Tara Ruhl (Jackson, MI Head Start), Michelle Crossley (Jackson, MI Head Start), Marilyn Dolbeare-Matthews (Frederick County Public Schools, Maryland), Deborah Harvey (Department of Defense Schools), Karla Lerma (Palm Beach County, Florida), and Mitch Bobrick (Palm Beach County, Florida).

In addition, we received advice and assistance from Melissa Shamblott (St. Paul, MN Public Schools), Jonathan Fribley (MN Department of Children, Families, and Learning), Jeannie Chaffins and Janet Baldwin of 8CAP Head Start (Greenville, MI), Jackie Barber, Brenda Webster, Cindy Rowe, and Natalie Guy-Hazard of the Community Action Agency Head Start (Jackson, MI), and Elizabeth Servidio (Madison, AL). Additional comments were provided by Vicky Milner (DeWitt, MI Public Schools), Marcy Borchers, Mary Salman, Kim Hoffmann, and Bob Charters (Tri County Head Start, Paw Paw, MI), Mary Brandeau and Lana Tatom (Willow Run, MI, Public Schools), Marie McCabe-Johnson (Ann Arbor, MI), Emily Ternes (New Beginnings Academy, Ypsilanti, MI), and Nona Gibbs (Flint, MI).

Critical to the production of this work was Margaret FitzGerald of Metaphor Marketing, who worked with us through every step of generating ideas, developing prototypes, and design and production. Her efforts were critical to the success of these materials. She was assisted by Paula Bousley, who provided invaluable production support and helped the authors in numerous ways. Nancy Booth provided us with extremely valuable copyediting assistance.

Others who made numerous essential contributions included Carla Christensen, Ruth Wollin, and other staff at Rebus Inc and at Print-Tech, Inc. Patty Humphrey's support was also of great value to the authors in producing early versions of the guidelines.

Finally, the fourth edition owes an immense debt of gratitude to the thousands of teachers who have used Work Sampling over the years and who shared their thoughts, preferences, dislikes, and hopes. We have tried to listen to these colleagues and to represent their opinions as faithfully as possible in this new edition.

Third Edition:

This work was supported in part by a grant from the John D. and Catherine T. MacArthur Foundation awarded to Samuel J. Meisels. It was also assisted by support from the Brattleboro (VT) Follow Through Program and other sources.

In particular, we wish to thank the following individuals for their valuable suggestions and feedback:

From Brattleboro (VT) Public Schools: Jean Albee, Pam Becker, Patricia Berger, Kathy Ernst, Margerie Guthrie, Deborah Hall, Judie Jerald, Janis Kiehle, Polly Kurty, Donna Natowich, Charlotte Stetson, and Linn Wilson; From Bank Street College of Education (NYC): Joan Cenedella, Judith Gold, and Elizabeth Servidio; From Gilman School, Baltimore (MD): Wickes MacColl; From Park School, Baltimore (MD): Sharon Pula; From Wellesley (MA) Public Schools: Laura Thorpe Katz; From District of Columbia Public Schools: Austine Fowler, Martha Hansen, and Parker Anderson; From Pittsburgh (PA) Public Schools: Diane Briars and Joanne Eresh.

Teachers and staff from the following districts have played an ongoing role in the development of Work Sampling: Willow Run (MI) Community Schools and Massachusetts Project Impact, including the districts of Agawam, Boston, Cambridge, Lynn, Lynn Economic Opportunity Head Start, Old Rochester, Pioneer Valley, and Somerset.

Teachers from the folowing school districts were instrumental in the early development of Work Sampling: Dexter (MI) Public Schools, Davison (MI) Public Schools, Flint (MI) Public Schools, Northview (MI) Public Schools, and Fort Worth (TX) Independent School District.

Grateful acknowledgement is made to our colleague Aviva Dorfman, who reviewed every element of the Guidelines and who contributed substantially to them in many ways. In addition, we are extremely grateful to Joni Block of the Massachusetts Department of Education, Diane Trister Dodge of Teaching Strategies, Inc., Donna Bickel of the Pittsburgh Public Schools, Lauren Ashley of the Brattleboro Public Schools, and our Work Sampling colleagues who contributed to this effort, particularly Regena Fails and Sylvia Jones. Dorothy Steele made major contributions to the original formulation of the Work Sampling System. Others without whom this work could not have taken place include June Patterson, Toni Bickart, Sally Provence, and Irving Marsden. Sue Kelley, Jan Blomberg, Sally Atkins-Burnett, Pat McMahon, and Kris Kasperski of the University of Michigan assisted the project in countless ways. Finally, we are indebted to Tiff Crutchfield of Mode Design whose remarkable assistance in design, layout, and production has resulted in both the attractive appearance and systemic integrity of the Work Sampling materials.

Margo Dichtelmiller
Judy Jablon
Dot Marsden
Sam Meisels